FINDING
NORTH JERSEY

FINDING
NORTH JERSEY

PLACE, PASSAGE, EXPERIENCE

JAMES W. MARCUM

THE
History
PRESS

Published by The History Press
Charleston, SC 29403
www.historypress.net

Copyright © 2012 by James W. Marcum
All rights reserved

Cover images are turn-of-the-century postcards.

First published 2012

Manufactured in the United States

ISBN 978.1.60949.811.5
Library of Congress CIP data applied for.

CONTENTS

PREFACE

Writing *Finding North Jersey* was a labor of love for a Southwest transplant who has lived in New Jersey for a decade. You may think it presumptuous of me for thinking that I have something to offer natives and long-term residents. But newcomers sometimes see things that natives take for granted, and that is why new residents in a region or country sometimes become successful innovators or pioneers. North Jersey is no exception. This particular newcomer has developed a distinct perspective, and so I proceed without trepidation.

For my wife Becky and me, this is a special place. Here we find the openness, dynamism, diversity, standard of living, accessibility to the megalopolis that is New York and the surprisingly varied ecology of North Jersey to be a constant revelation and source of delight. I became intrigued with the area while working for Fairleigh Dickinson University, and since then, I have become steadily more engrossed in studying the character of the region and exploring its history, economy, culture and geography. But those are only starting points for understanding what defines a place.

The era in which I grew up was completely different from today. At that time, history was primarily about politics, with extensions into economics and war, and people were different. They belonged to nations and states; worked for long-lasting organizations that were either public or private; lived in suburbs or communities with people very much like themselves; were part of a traditional family or lived alone; and either went to college or didn't and, accordingly, spent their lives in white-collar or blue-collar work.

Traditional history—at least, before the influence of the Annales school of social history—required finding out what the main actors, primarily political actors, were doing. Usually documents were available, either in print collections or in archives, to facilitate such research. And the story was reasonably simple to reconstruct and narrate.

Finding North Jersey turned out to be something else entirely. Much had changed over the years, and I set out to understand this new and different place where I now live. And I learned that the story goes beyond politics and economics of the place; it is about a society that is far more complex than it was a few decades ago. This age of information has produced a very different world politically, economically, socially and organizationally. Society is now networked in ways that make many of our working assumptions about how things really work misleading, which raises questions about the validity and utility of many of our fundamental institutions, starting with the territorial-political state. There are many more people here now, and a lot more of them are involved in the affairs of the day through new communications and media.

INQUIRY

This project did not begin with the idea of telling a specific story; it began as a quest for answers to questions that emerged after spending a decade living in the region. The questions guided the process, and the outcome was determined when the answers satisfied the inquirer. Some of these questions can be answered quickly while others require extensive exploration and may remain unsettled and emergent. While researching, a different method of learning and investigation emerged—the inquiry method. Rather than starting with the enormous library of books and documents and data and then sorting through and extracting the meaning of it all, I started by asking questions and then sought out the answers. There is too much information today for a short book that seeks to interpret a complex topic from a wide, multidisciplinary perspective.

THE QUESTIONS

Each question will be addressed in a chapter of the book. For each question, I have listed one to several related questions asked in an attempt to understand and interpret the area we call North Jersey.

1. WHERE IS NORTH JERSEY? Is it the northern half of the state, the area north of Interstate 195? If so, that would mean the region encompasses thirteen of the state's twenty-one counties. But residents of Central Jersey reject that description, for Central Jersey forms a complicated region, ranging from urban tenements to the rural mountains of the northwest Highlands. Such variety complicates finding unique characteristics for the North Jersey region. Other definitions simplify the matter and prove more helpful. Is North Jersey simply part of New York? Unquestionably, the city's influence, proximity and interdependence suggest that it is. Does that determine the nature of the region? Or are other factors more important? This question will continually come up throughout our exploration, but many people in the area believe that the region is essentially a collection of suburbs that are a part of New York City, often called Gotham for short.

2. WHO ARE THE PEOPLE OF NORTH JERSEY? Who lives here? Where did they come from? Where are they going? What are they trying to do? North Jersey has continuously been the destination for waves of immigrants from all parts of the world. Additionally, many people move to North Jersey from other parts of the United States. The area is therefore remarkably diverse, and coping with that diversity has been a constant challenge in recent years.

3. WHY IS NORTH JERSEY DIFFERENT? Why are there no great cities and why are there so many towns with fewer than two thousand people? Several stories from both the past and present will help us understand, as will discussions of disputes and divisions, visions and innovations, New York imperialism and home rule.

4. IS NORTH JERSEY SIMPLY SUBURBAN? What is the pattern of living in the area? Why is it characterized as classic suburbia with perpetual sprawl and decaying cities? Is it actually different from other suburbs in the United States? Who will determine the next style of living? Will it be realtors, builders or chambers of commerce? Or will it be community

groups, grass-roots organizations and urban planners? Or could it be the ordinary people living out their lives and pursuing their dreams without worrying about these matters?

5. How Did North Jersey Become What It Is Today? How can the dynamism of North Jersey be explained? Many point to location and transportation. Being part of the New York–Philadelphia route clearly played a major historical role in shaping North Jersey. What led to the construction of railroads, expressways, tunnels and bridges? What impact did these infrastructures have? What mix of politics created them and how did they affect the region's development and prosperity? Is North Jersey essentially a passage to somewhere else?

6. How Has North Jersey Changed? Has it changed? Is it a place that is settled and enduring? Or is it constantly changing? A place has meaning; it holds onto the emotions of its residents. Is that true of North Jersey?

These questions essentially boil down to one: Is North Jersey characterized by adaptation or innovation? That leads us to wonder whether the region is simply subject to and forced to adapt to outside forces (primarily New York City), location, commerce and ecology. If not, then have its people steadily struggled to manage those factors, overcome obstacles and setbacks, set their own agenda and deal with the forces that would determine their fate? And that leads to another question: Is North Jersey actually a region distinctive from its surroundings and neighbors?

There is extensive data, fine scholarship and additional evidence that can be gleaned from novels, stories, songs, films and popular culture addressing the issues of place, work and quality of life in North Jersey. But determining the location, development and distinctive character of the region in the public mind requires a story and its acceptance by many people. The ultimate goal of this book is to find out not only what North Jersey is today but also what it can become.

This study is not intended to be definitive. All of the questions considered here warrant a more thorough study. But this book presents answers to *my* questions, and once I found these answers, I moved on. I look forward to further studies by those who seek definitive answers to the more specific questions and issues.

ACKNOWLEDGEMENTS

My thanks and appreciation go to the libraries that provided the support and information needed to write this book: Morris County Library, Montville Township Public Library and Morristown Morris Township Public Library, particularly its North Jersey History Center. Queens College's Rosenthal Library also provided many sources. The Special Collections and Archives branch of Alexander Library at Rutgers University allowed me to access a number of needed images, as did the New Jersey Room of the Jersey City Public Library. A special thanks to Danny Klein, who works at the New Jersey Room, for his assistance.

The Old Book Shop in Morristown proved to be a valuable source. Thank you Frank Galardi of Lincoln Park; Richard Goerner; and Greg Fallon. Also, special thanks to Elwood (Woody) Kerkeslager of Madison, New Jersey. Of course, the wisest advice and best resources cannot guarantee freedom from error. I claim those for myself.

And always, thanks to my support system, my wife, Becky.

CHAPTER 1

WHERE IS NORTH JERSEY?

*There's a larger issue shaping the people of New Jersey, and that is…just about
everyone from the Garden State wants to escape.*
—*K. Buckley*

Location is a key part of explaining and understanding the development
of North Jersey as a special place. It was one of the original thirteen
states and has fertile land that supports agriculture, as well as ample forests
for fuel and rivers for power and transport. It is also near New York—the
"great city" of the nation. Many agree that there are two parts to the state:
the north and the south. The U.S. census's description of the New York and
Philadelphia metropolitan areas supports this regional division of the state
in that way. Others claim there is a third Jersey—Central Jersey. In his book
A Geography of New Jersey, Geographer Charles Stansfield describes seven
regions, adding the Northwestern Highlands, the Pinelands, the Seashore
and a Southwest Farm Belt to the main three. Henry Charles Beck's *Tales
and Towns of Northern New Jersey* defines North Jersey as a state made up
of five counties: Bergen, Passaic, Morris, Essex and Hudson. Still others
divide the state further. For instance, there is a commercial effort in the
Northwest New Jersey Skylands area to promote itself as a tri-county
tourist destination (which includes Sussex, Warren and Hunterdon).
Understanding these various divisions requires a few definitions, and
putting the issue in the larger context of globalization and human society
helps to frame the issues driving this book. When done, we will provide

a case that North Jersey is a place that is distinctive from the rest of New Jersey as well as New York.

CHOOSE ONE

All of the previous descriptions suggest that pinpointing precisely where North Jersey is located is complicated. North Jersey is an informal term that, above all, suggests a direction. From a purely geographic perspective, it would be the northern half of the state. The state itself is neatly divided by Interstate 195, which runs eastward from Trenton to the shore. Defining North Jersey in this manner separates the northern and southern parts of the state into roughly equal parts in terms of land. However, that doesn't mean the two are equal in other ways. The majority of the state's population resides in the northern thirteen counties and totals approximately 6.37 million (72.5 percent of the population). Consequently, North Jersey has more towns, businesses and history. According to Virginia Faulkner, a Morristown bookseller, there are three or four books that discuss the towns, people and events of the north for each book on South Jersey communities. But interestingly, there are more active organizations, books, pamphlets and events emphasizing the South Jersey character as a region with its slower pace, its proximity to Philadelphia and its distinctiveness from North Jersey.

There are problems, however, in designating all areas above I-195 as North Jersey. People who live in the western and more mountainous part of the state in Sussex, Hunterdon and Warren Counties do not identity themselves as part of North Jersey. The title of a folklore program in the western Highlands area reads "No Exit Numbers," highlighting the fact that neither the New Jersey Turnpike nor the Garden State Parkway cuts through the area. More agricultural and rural, the small towns of these counties do not share the crowded and rapid pace of cities in the northern part of the state, and local taxes are less burdensome. Mercer and parts of Middlesex County consider themselves distinct from "North Jersey" and identify themselves as part of Central Jersey. These two counties, which are centered around the high-tech corridor that stretches along Highway 1 between Rutgers University in New Brunswick and Princeton, serve as a partition between North and South Jersey. For the purpose of this book, however, we will refer to the entire area north of Trenton and I-195 as Greater New Jersey.

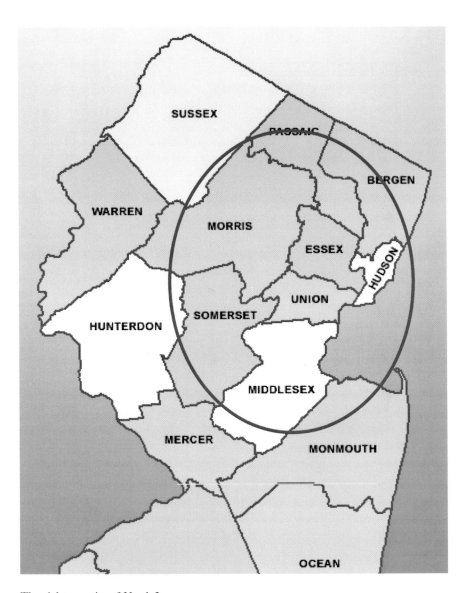

The eight counties of North Jersey.

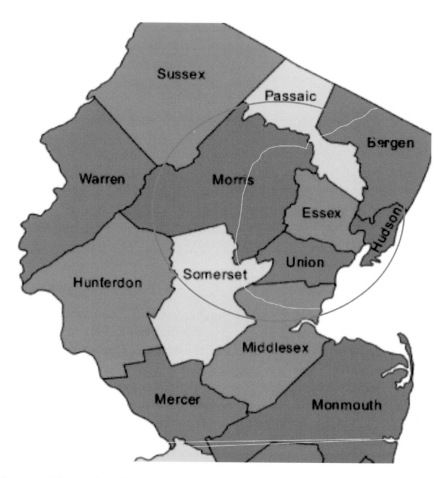

Interstate 297 runs through or surrounds all eight North Jersey counties.

Greater North Jersey is the area north of Interstate 195.

PART OF NEW YORK?

What role does New York City play in the life of North Jersey? This is a central issue to identifying North Jersey, one that we will return to frequently. Dennis Gale, a retired Rutgers political science professor, refers to Bergen, Hudson, Essex, Union and Passaic Counties, located in the northeast part of the state, as "Greater New Jersey." He argues that this area is part of suburban New York, akin to four of the city's outer boroughs (Staten Island, the Bronx, Brooklyn and Queens). He suggests that the region "cannot be understood apart from its network of relationships with New York City." The millions of commuters who travel to New York every year are one element of "interactive economic regions inconvenienced by multiple politics."

Unquestionably, the city's influence on and connections to North Jersey, as well as the two areas' interdependence, support Gale's argument. The number of commuters and the reliance on the entertainment New York City provides—museums, sports teams and so forth—serve as evidence. Because of its proximity to New York City, North Jersey has a population density four times that of the rest of the state. Over the course of one hundred years, the area's population rose dramatically.

Years	"Greater New Jersey" Population
1850	160,846
1900	1,078,097
1950	2,831,756

Other factors come into play, however. The first great population spurt occurred during the Industrial Revolution. Paterson, located in Passaic County, was the country's first planned industrial city and was founded based on the economic development proposals of Alexander Hamilton. Hamilton saw the power of Paterson's Great Falls as a source of energy that was quite accessible from New York. Paterson ultimately realized his dream of an industrial center, but Newark in nearby Essex County developed more quickly as a major industrial area, producing a wide range of goods for the region and the nation throughout the late nineteenth century and well into the twentieth. Additionally, there were plants and companies in Elizabeth, Hoboken, Bayonne and Jersey City that made the region economically

New York City skyline from Bayonne, New Jersey. *Photo by author.*

productive and brought many emigrants from Europe and beyond who were seeking a better life.

Gale's "Greater New Jersey" is useful, but it is a bit narrow for our purposes, and we will use the idea more as a sounding board than as an actual definition in identifying North Jersey. Additionally, it should not be confused with our use of Greater North Jersey for the entire northern half of the state.

It is necessary to note that New Jersey's struggles with New York have impacted the region as well. For years, the state did not have a defined northern border. During the Revolutionary War, there were repeated raids conducted by New Yorkers that were substantial enough to be labeled "border wars" by some. These conflicts resulted in New Yorkers claiming and occupying New Jersey land. It took quite some time and effort for the boundary between the two states to be clearly defined and recognized.

New York Imperialism

The question of whether New York sought to dominate or even acquire New Jersey occasionally arises. The conflict over the border can be traced back to the moment when James Stuart casually ripped Staten Island away from its geographic locale to pacify certain grievances regarding New Jersey's creation following the ouster of the Dutch from New Amsterdam. This would be a long-term grievance and wasn't helped by royal governors who were responsible for both colonies but based in New York. There were occasional armed invasions from New York into the northern part of New Jersey, usually under some sort of pretense regarding control of land or rivers. Colonial governors imposed import duties on New Jersey goods during the late 1700s, which fed fear of large-state dominance. During the nineteenth century, railroad monopolies fell under the influence of New York investors. New York's claim to both sides of the Hudson River led to numerous business schemes and counter schemes, as well as the occasional armed skirmish. New Yorkers stubbornly refused to recognize Jersey interests in regard to Ellis Island, and this only caused more discord between the two states. That quarrel was finally resolved in 1998, when the Supreme Court handed down a decision awarding most of Ellis Island to New Jersey. Prior to 1950, the U.S. census lumped North Jersey into a larger New York suburban region that also included western Connecticut. This was updated to a Standard Metropolitan Statistical Area (SMSA) in 1960.

Another example of seemingly imperialist activity is the states' past struggle to control the ridge along the Hudson River's western shore. Known as Bergen Hill or the Palisades, this ridge stretches some twenty miles from Jersey City into the lower part of New York State and was a very real obstacle in linking roads and other infrastructures through New Jersey to Philadelphia. At one point, the New York–controlled Erie Railroad tried to block access to the newer Lackawanna Railroad that cut through Bergen Hill. The privileged and powerful Camden & Amboy Railroad eventually came under control of New York interests. All these events were unlikely the product of an intentional "imperialist" effort or plan, but suspicious minds argue otherwise.

There is no question that North Jersey depends on New York; rather, the question is *to what extent* does it depend on New York? While New Jersey experienced a slow and steady growth, New York grew at an exponentially fast rate, not only in population but also in commerce and financial power.

In 1800, New York's port controlled less than 10 percent of America's foreign trade; by 1870, it controlled over 50 percent and was buttressed by the creation of the Erie Canal. But in reality, New York depends as much on North Jersey as North Jersey depends on New York. New York proudly calls itself the Empire State, and although it is uncertain where this moniker actually came from, most believe it stems from early nineteenth-century celebrations of the state surpassing Virginia in population, making it the largest state in the Union. Neighboring areas—namely Canada, Connecticut and especially North Jersey—see the Empire State building in Manhattan as a symbol of this ambition to be dominant. In their eyes, the Empire State represents an arrogant intent to politically and economically control the area.

Economics was a larger issue. Sometime during the Industrial Revolution, business leaders developed a new attitude and began focusing less on civic capitalism and more on something entirely new, described by some as national or corporate capitalism. Earlier, it was entrepreneurs who started their own businesses and banded together with others to bolster their power, strengthening their community in the process. Such people made Trenton a leading commercial city in America during the 1880s. But when financial capital came into play, things changed. Finance, marketing and management took control, and the fate of local manufacturers fell into the hands of corporate offices, not just in Trenton but nationwide. Place was no longer important. Trenton slowly declined and never recovered. Conversely, New York became, and still is, the nation's leading financial center. New York's drive to expand that capital in the nineteenth century and after was not so much intentional empire building as it was a quest for profit.

A WORKING DEFINITION

There is a descriptor used in business circles labeling the five "Greater New Jersey counties" (and additionally Middlesex, Morris and Somerset Counties) as "economic" North Jersey. This configuration includes a second ring of "suburbs" that succeeded the core group. We might label this area as the I-287 enclave since that thoroughfare loops through Bergen, Passaic, Morris, Somerset and Middlesex Counties and encloses the older urban counties of Hudson, Essex and Union. This gives us a total of eight counties that have much more in common than economics. Physically, the land is primarily piedmont, hilly or flat but lacking mountains or shoreline. All eight counties are part of metropolitan regions and have relatively large populations, each averaging over 500,000 people. There are some large towns, a few small cities (such as Newark, Jersey City, Elizabeth and Paterson) and over two hundred municipalities. That averages out to twenty-eight municipalities per county, which is excessive by national standards. Most of these smaller towns have municipal governments with mayors, city managers, police and fire chiefs and school superintendents, but overall, the standard of living in the region is high, and residents pay large taxes.

The figures are a bit misleading. Bergen County alone has 905,116 people (according to the 2010 census) and seventy-two municipalities, while Somerset County has a population of 323,444 and twenty-one municipalities. But remarkably, all (save Hudson County) have significant stretches of preserved woodlands or wetlands, which makes all of these counties unique despite the high population density.

Below are the counties listed from north to south, along with their populations, square mileage and significant towns.

County	Population (2010 census)	Square Miles	County Seat	Important Towns
Bergen	905,116	246.75	Hackensack	Fort Lee
Passaic	501,226	193.81	Paterson*	Wayne
Hudson	634,266	62.24	Jersey City*	Bayonne, Hoboken
Essex	783,969	129.56	Newark*	East Orange, Irvington
Morris	492,276	481.23	Morristown	Parsippany
Union	536,499	103.40	Elizabeth*	Union
Somerset	323,444	304.99	Somerville	
Middlesex	809,858	322.56	New Brunswick	Edison,* Woodbridge

Total   4,986,653   1,844.54

* Cities with a population greater than 100,000

In terms of area, this region makes up only 21 percent of the state's 8,721 square miles, yet 56.7 percent of the state's population lives here. Furthermore, New Jersey is the most densely populated state in the nation and is in global competition with Bangladesh and the city-state of Singapore for most densely populated state.

Distinguishing North Jersey from the rest of the state changes some realities but not all. Certainly, it is recognized as different from South Jersey. Indeed, it has more in common with New York than it does the more rural, suburban and agricultural southern part of the state. Additionally, New Jersey has the second-highest populations by percentage of Jews (after New York) and Muslims (after Michigan) in the United States and ranks third in population percentage of Italians, Indians and Koreans. The great bulk of these people live in North Jersey. By itself, North Jersey would rank as the second-smallest state after Rhode Island, but the area houses nearly five times the number of people. But this inspires the question of whether North Jerseyans themselves view their area as such an exceptional and diverse place. To answer that, we will have to return to Gale.

THE IMAGE PROBLEM

In *Greater New Jersey*, Gale discusses the problem of North Jersey's image. He first points out how North Jersey's identity is diluted as a result of its dependence on New York television stations for network news and programming. New Jersey has no commercial TV station, and its public television station, NJN, recently had to seek new management when the financially strapped state pulled its support. The *Star Ledger* reported that New York station WNET's takeover of the station ended forty years of focused New Jersey political reporting and continues to be a cause of concern about the extent and depth of coverage of the state's politics.

The absence of a dominating city means the absence of a dominating state newspaper. The *Bergen Record* is strong in the far north, particularly in Bergen County, and the *Star Ledger* is a good paper that covers North Jersey and beyond, but the paper struggles for adequate support beyond its base in Newark. The reality is that most Jerseyans know more about New York politics and that city's mayor than they do about important state political figures, with the possible exception of the governor. The absence of a strong media presence has profound importance in that the treatment of issues is scattered among various media outlets on both sides of the Hudson River, and rarely does an issue beyond state politics become critical in the minds of the people of the state. Today, there are major sports franchises based in the Meadowlands (New York Giants and New York Jets) and in Newark (New Jersey Devils). The Nets' move from Rutherford to Brooklyn serves as further evidence of the lack of commitment on the part of professional sports teams toward the area and the people of New Jersey to support local teams. Indeed, most major-league teams in the area identify themselves as New York based.

If the lack of a major city or other powerful image isn't enough of a problem, there are additional factors that keep North Jersey from being seen in a positive light. First, there is the enduring legacy of crime families and political corruption. The latter will be discussed more in a later chapter, but the mafia stereotype is branded in the minds of Americans, thanks in part to mafia movies and television shows such as *The Sopranos*. The Newark riots of 1967 and the city's ongoing troubles with violent crime also affect North Jersey's image, as well as the state's.

Finally, Gale offers a collection of people and things that strictly belong to New Jersey, subdivided into three categories: native celebrities, from Frank Sinatra to Bruce Springsteen; innovations such as "edge cities"; and inventors and scientists, such as Thomas Edison and Albert Einstein. According to Gale, these offer a more polished image for New Jersey. However, the prevalence of corruption, bad politics, ineffective and costly governance and urban crime all contribute to North Jersey's less-than-stellar reputation.

One point Gale overlooks that undermines his presentation of close ties with New York is what we've already labeled New York imperialism. From colonial times to very recently, New York interests have endeavored to control or influence Jersey's political and economical affairs. I have introduced this theme already, but the point needs to be discussed more thoroughly. A write-up describing the background and origins of the 1960s pop group Frankie Valli and the Four Seasons accompanied the launch of the wildly popular Broadway show *Jersey Boys* in 2005. The article points out that the group received little attention from the elitist impresarios of New York despite the fact the group enjoyed decades of enormous national success. The group appealed to blue-collar working-class people but could not compete with the icons of the civil rights and anti-war movements nor the influence of drugs grabbing the attention of the media, and they therefore received very little recognition from the recording industry. Despite his eventual success, Frank Sinatra had his troubles with the media early in his career. It took Bruce Springsteen and his rock music to finally establish a positive Jersey cultural icon.

The point is not an isolated one. In an essay published in the *Wall Street Journal,* one critic described the situation as "the hidden state of culture." According to the article, buried beneath the state's fractured personality and jumble of contrasts is a "remarkable harvest of talent" and a veritable "cultural epicenter." This recognition, however, comes late, but that will be discussed in a later chapter.

Distance

As previously mentioned, North Jersey is the most densely populated area in the state, and for that reason, the actual distance between people needs to be considered. The idea is known as proxemics and deals with proximity (as the name suggests) and space different cultures expect in interpersonal relationships. Social theorists claim that overcrowding produces unsocial and violent behavior. Certainly, this is something to keep in mind as a factor in understanding North Jersey today, as well as its past, before progressive social policy gained traction in the twentieth century. The negative response to overcrowding and the dumping of foul waste material has been observed in both humans and animals. Public space in downtown areas varies from Spanish town squares to allowances for foot traffic in Paris and Venice, to crowded tenements in Jersey City. The demands of the automobile have complicated the matter significantly, disrupting neighborhoods and local traffic patterns. North Jersey provides an important testing ground for the theory, though with only a few violent exceptions such as the 1967 Newark riot, it seems that a dense mixture of cultures and ethnic groups and pollution is not necessarily combustible. To what can we credit this good news? Does the North Jersey experience substantiate or discredit the theory?

A GLOBAL PLACE

In the time of global communication, commerce and competition, a region is no longer determined to be solely part of a state or nation. For decades, economists have expounded on globalization and its impact on local areas. The term is used broadly but is meant to signal the impact of multinational corporations on business at all levels, from the local to the national and even regional. The shift in politics during the 1980s freed corporations from being tied to a place, and they quickly made arrangements to move money, factories and some corporate headquarters to places with low tax rates, little governmental oversight, rock-bottom labor rates and minimal worker protections. Facilities—mostly manufacturing plants—were quickly moved to Mexico, the Caribbean, the Pacific Rim and China, and in each of these places, the cost of labor was a fraction of what American companies paid in wages. Most northern textile plants had already moved to the southern United States by the early 1970s, and in the 1980s, many again made the jump to areas that had even lower costs. The industrial decline, evidenced by the hollowing out of downtown urban areas, accelerated and was spurred in part by events in Detroit and Newark, where racial tension had reached an all-time high.

Thomas Friedman, a seasoned and respected correspondent for the *New York Times*, hit the bestseller list in 2006 with *The World Is Flat*, which was a more extensive version of his influential book *The Lexus and the Olive Tree*, an early exposition on global business and its consequences. Vivid anecdotes, interviews with corporate and political headliners and a compelling narrative by familiar "talking heads" persuaded many thoughtful people to buy into his conviction that globalization was an accomplished reality and the only choice remaining was to climb aboard the train or fall by the wayside.

The notion of globalization became very popular in academic circles and was avidly discussed in the media and on college campuses in the 1980s. One example is an academic study of three towns in Upstate New York that fell on hard times in the years after 1970. Between the years 1850 and 1950, Utica, Hartwick and Cooperstown flourished. Connecting the Great Lakes region with the Hudson River near Albany, the Erie Canal made the port of New York a dominant trade hub and commercial center. Utica in particular benefited from the impact of the canal; not long after the canal opened, its population soared to 100,000. However, when General Electric and other firms pulled out of the area and moved their operations to the South or overseas, 40,000 people lost their jobs. The benefits enjoyed by the three towns disappeared, and all had to try to reinvent themselves. According to author Alexander Thomas, this was not only a consequence of New York having finance capital but also a result of trade expansion and relations with other parts of the country (and globe), as well as a general decline in the city's reliance on its "hinterlands" for its growth and development. Other places and companies farther away offered more appealing opportunities for investment and business expansion than Upstate New York. New shopping malls decimated Utica's downtown. All three towns had to try to reinvent themselves. The powerful financial presence of New York caused the decline of many towns and regions during the late twentieth century, especially those in North Jersey. David Harvey adds that capital flows and the manipulation of capital by central bankers and financiers render state action less important to the business scene, particularly for manufacturing. For instance, capital led the shift from the production-centered activity of agriculture and early industry to today's consumer economy and, additionally, allowed companies to establish their manufactures and enterprises in faraway places.

But is this a good thing? In *World 3.0*, Pankaj Ghemawat shows that the opening of borders and reduction of tariffs enhance the flow of information, goods and services that can meliorate areas that have suffered long-standing episodes of famine, disease and even war. This suggests that national and state frontiers matter less than before, but place and distance still matter, and that makes the importance of locale even greater. Mesoarrangements (intermediate arrangements between local and state levels) could be viable options for dealing with a number of North Jersey's problems, as will be discussed in a later chapter. New York's relationship with North Jersey is casual and piecemeal—focused and institutionalized. Therefore, thinking on a global scale and acting on a local level remain appropriate for the day Ghemawat labels "semi-globalization." North Jersey is a territory, even if it is not formally organized as such, and a tension lies quietly, or arises vigorously, between the territory of a region and the flows of global capital. North Jersey's position in this global world of flows becomes more complex than mere dependence on New York. For example, in its unceasing quest for opportunity and profit, Wall Street occasionally turns its attention to the area. But North Jersey is mature, developed and dense. Just as national corporations seek far more exciting financial possibilities elsewhere, from Middle East oil reserves to Chinese marketplaces, corporate and business leaders in North Jersey sometimes focus on New York.

SOCIAL FACTORS

Geography and location have been the main focus of this chapter thus far. To reemphasize, globalization diminishes the importance of place. As David Harvey explains in *The Urbanization of Capital*, capital flows provide the force behind the massive development of infrastructure and suburbs that have attracted capital investments for most of the twentieth century, creating the materialist consumer society that brought apparent prosperity to a much larger share of American society we know as the middle class. But Harvey also acknowledges the role of geography and place in human affairs. The local, spatial fixes of societies create a world of diversity. The enduring power of landownership and management is largely overlooked by pundits of globalization, which is a problem since landownership can amount to as much as 40 percent of a country's economic activity.

The social impulse of humanity is also a factor. People require human interaction. We do not like to be alone for very long, and those who lack sufficient human contact develop serious pathologies. Humans have therefore formed increasingly larger groups over time, starting with hunter-gatherer groups in early human history. These groups expanded to become farming communities during the Agricultural Revolution. With the emergence of cities came greater stratification of markets and classes, and industrialism further complicated social and work interactions as cities and commerce became steadily more important. Transportation and communication improvements also increased the number of humans and allowed for more diversity in any given area. With its diverse economy and stubborn devotion to small-town living spaces, North Jersey is a marvelous laboratory for many of the most significant issues and problems facing American society today, including mesolevel political arrangements. But additional information is required for that discussion.

JUST NORTH JERSEY

To close this chapter, let's address one key question. Many writers, as well as the U.S. census, consider North Jersey to be part of New York, specifically the New York Metropolitan District. Certainly, the two are tied together commercially and culturally, as aforementioned. But North Jersey, while distinctive from the state of New Jersey, is also separated from New York by a great river, political jurisdictions and history. Meanwhile, its economy is more focused on the nation and globe today than it is on Manhattan. Here is a little data to illustrate:

NORTH JERSEY COUNTY TO COUNTY WORKER FLOW (2000 U.S. CENSUS)

Residence	Workplace				
County	Manhattan (New York County)	Home County	Other N°J Counties	Total in North Jersey	Workforce Total
Bergen	61,300	246,000	123,400	369,400	430,700
Essex	28,100	175,200	135,500	310,700	338,800
Hudson	58,400	121,400	72,100	193,500	251,900
Middlesex	25,800	201,800	79,100	280,900	305,700
Morris	11,500	138,700	83,900	222,600	234,100
Passaic	8,400	95,800	62,400	158,200	166,600
Somerset	6,200	66,300	56,700	123,000	129,200
Union	16,300	113,300	86,100	199,400	215,700
TOTAL	216,000	1,158,500	699,200	1,857,700	2,073,700

These workforce figures include North Jersey inhabitants working in North Jersey or Manhattan. Approximately 10 percent of North Jersey workers commute to New York City. That is less than the 15 percent historically used by the census to designate the economic integration in the SMSA and well below the 25 percent utilized as the threshold today. Over half of the people that compose the area's workforce are employed in their home county. Of the remaining half, for each commuter to New York, more than three workers commute to another North Jersey county. Location is a major reality shaping North Jersey, but with the exception of Hudson County (26 percent of whom are Manhattan commuters), North Jersey does not meet the standards required of the SMSA and, therefore, is not simply part of New York.

CHAPTER 2

WHO IS NORTH JERSEY?

To me, Hoboken's story [is] *contrasting the early German and Irish influences thrust from memory by the mixture of nationalities which cluster in cities across the land*
—*H.C. Beck*

Most writers of the New Jersey experience mention the relatively large population over a relatively small portion of land and the diversity of its people. Certainly, there is little to dispute on the point. But what are the causes and practical consequences of that density and diversity? What does it mean for North Jersey today and in the future? Plausible answers can be found in examining the region's population and history.

NATIVES

The Lenni Lenape or Delaware Indians, a major Algonquian tribe and relatively peaceful people, first populated the area we now know as North Jersey. These tribes grew maize and tobacco and were also hunter-gatherers, and both of these methods for acquiring food allowed the tribes to grow and support themselves. They moved to their semi-permanent villages in the fall and spring and migrated to shore for the summer, where they caught fish and clams and enjoyed the cool water. The Algonquians also engaged in trade with many other tribes. Tribal membership was determined by matrilineal descent, and women collectively "owned" the land on behalf of the tribe. After marrying, men usually moved in with their wives' families to settle. The natives' peaceful ways, however, did not serve them well against their warlike Iroquois neighbors and European settlers, and they were steadily pushed farther west, and only a scattered few ultimately remained in their local territories.

American Indian–European relations involved more than war and destruction emphasized in history books. The early settlers were few and scattered, and for the most part, they found it far better to get along with the natives than to provoke trouble by imposing their will or faith. But getting along took effort from both sides. The difference in appearance, dress, customs and behavior inspired curiosity as well as fear and suspicion. Troubles were then unavoidable, and many settlers were taken captive in Indian raids. There were some settlers who chose to remain with the Indians rather than returning to their European-style settlements, however, and there were also a few cases where Indians chose to remain as part of white society if they had the choice of returning to their people. But of course, these natives and those who didn't join white society were still susceptible to contagions the European immigrants brought with them.

The Lenni Lenape were fortunate to live in a region that was relatively rich in game and fish and had a variety of vegetation, woodlands and arable land. They were, however, unfortunate in that they lived in a place that attracted aggressive native tribes and European colonists. These advantages and disadvantages set a pattern that explains much about what happened to the early peoples and to waves of settlers as one succeeded the other.

EARLY SETTLERS

The first waves of settlers to present-day North Jersey were Dutch and English. Because the two nationalities shared a Protestant heritage, they got along relatively well. English settlers, who were more aristocratic, settled primarily on the better agricultural lands in the southwest area of the region, while Scots-Irish settlers settled in the more rural areas with the Dutch. In addition to working the land, the settlers practiced beekeeping and weaving, and they also made cider. Others set up sawmills or gristmills, particularly

Passaic River, Rutherford. Rivers facilitated the settlement and development of the region. *Postcard.*

in North Jersey where there were numerous rivers for power. There were also pockets of early Swedish settlers and German-speaking families, and while they did not always get along, they shared a religious heritage and North European origin. Their numbers were few, however, and mastery of the territory was shaky and far from complete for many years.

Early settlers soon learned that iron ore was readily available in the area; sometimes, it was just lying in sight on the ground. Iron production eventually became a substantial enterprise and was highly concentrated in the east part of North Jersey. Large ironworks were constructed, and they employed a considerable number of workers, indentured servants and even slaves to operate the works. Additionally, iron production required furnaces and forges and demanded a great deal of wood for fuel. In fact, it is estimated that North Jersey's ironworks used a thousand acres of trees annually. An iron plantation plan was developed, and it visualized an ideal twenty thousand acres, so that there would be regrowth to make the business sustainable. These plantations were scattered across the forest areas and were isolated from settlements and other farms. The establishment of ironworks in this region also necessitated the need for employee housing, as well as stores and farms for food production, and some plantations even provided a school and a church for their workers.

Above: Ringwood Manor in Passaic County is representative of the ironworks industry in North Jersey. *Photo by author.*

Left: Reenactor at a celebration at Ringwood Manor in July 2012. *Photo by author.*

IMMIGRATION IN WAVES

Immigration during the first half of the nineteenth century was slow and sporadic, and many of these newcomers were from Germany, where arable land was becoming scarce. Although most German immigrants set out for Ohio and Texas where land was vast and in great abundance, some did settle in New Jersey and worked digging canals, building railroads and joining the growing craft shops of Newark and Paterson. But things changed in the 1840s–50s. Famine in Ireland and turmoil in the Germanic states prompted an increase in emigration from both areas. Many Germans were accomplished farmers and brought their agricultural skills, as well as other skills, with them. Most of the Irish immigrants, conversely, turned to hard labor and were employed as canal diggers or worked for the railroads. And oftentimes, those who did come to America scouted for territory for their families who still resided in their native lands and would often write to their relatives about the success America offered.

The high tide of immigration started in the mid-1840s and lasted more than a decade. In the late nineteenth century, an estimated 40 percent of Ireland's population emigrated. According to statistics, 10 percent of Norwegians emigrated from their homeland, and a combined 7 percent of the British and Swedish populations left their countries. German arrivals in the United States had jumped from about 15,000 annually to 74,000 in 1847, and that number jumped again in 1854 to 215,000. The annual number of Irish immigrants coming into the United States peaked at 221,000 in 1851. Some of these newcomers quickly headed across the continent after hearing about the gold rush in the American West. Most, however, particularly those lacking the means to travel farther, settled in the Northeast and established communities, churches, festivals and newspapers in their native tongue.

This era, however, was not the time when the North Jersey, or even the New Jersey, experience was exceptional. According to the 1860 census, New Jersey ranked tenth among the states for number of immigrants; the leaders were larger eastern seaboard states, such as New York, Pennsylvania and Massachusetts, and also some midwestern states, namely Ohio, Illinois and Michigan.

Immigration reached its peak in the last third of the nineteenth century and in the first decades of the twentieth. The Industrial Revolution was continuing to develop across the country, and North Jersey became a center of activity. By 1900, some 120,000 or more Germans had arrived in the

United States, along with another 95,000 Irish immigrants. By that time, larger waves of people with much more diverse backgrounds were crowding in, bringing significant new challenges with them. The population of the state more than doubled between 1860 (672,000) and 1890 (1,445,000), and between 1850 and 1910, the population of New Jersey grew between 25 and 35 percent each decade. The increase in people, most of whom were from south and east Europe, required more land and more jobs, and in one form or another, both were provided but not at standards that would win the state any praise. In addition, very few of the newer immigrants knew English. Many lacked any marketable skill, lived in crowded city tenements and earned very little income. But somehow, the newcomers coped, and many thrived.

THE IMMIGRANT EXPERIENCE

Essays and memoirs from the nineteenth century are useful in navigating the complex and varied process of immigrants' adaptation to life in the United States. Newark, for example grew so rapidly that available housing could not keep pace. Some immigrants, particularly Italians, benefited from the population boom and found work in construction. But they, like other groups, typically lived for a time in boardinghouses or shared large residences, and

The Singer Manufacturing Plant, Elizabeth, circa 1905. *Postcard.*

most of these places lacked indoor toilets or running water. Several individuals and sometimes entire families shared a single room, which led to the rapid transmission of contagious diseases. Many immigrants lived for decades (some for a lifetime) without seeing a doctor. But the immigrant experience was not universal: each was unique, though many were defined by similar events. One memorable feature for many newcomers to Elizabeth, New Jersey, was the Singer Sewing Machine Company facility, which employed up to two thousand people and was known as a place where new arrivals could easily find work.

Many immigrants engaged in what is referred to as clustering by gathering in neighborhoods, cities and even regions. This provided some sense of familiarity and linguistic support as newcomers acclimated themselves to life in America. Some of these neighborhoods eventually became ghettos. Another trait was chain migration, where a village or family would send one of its own to immigrate and settle, and after that individual succeeded in establishing himself, he would send for a relative and eventually the rest of

This page and next: Newcomers gravitate to neighborhoods with stores that provide unique foods and services. Such offerings are apparent in Paterson, one of the most ethnically diverse cities in the nation. *Photo by author.*

the family. One Irish family sent a young married couple in 1921. The next year, the couple sent for a sister, and then for a brother and another sister in the years after that. By 1927, the couple's parents and their youngest child arrived. The stories are as numerous as the arrivals, but personal accounts all contain similarities and patterns. Here is breakdown of some ethnic groups that settled in North Jersey.

Irish

Irish immigrants were present in North Jersey as early as the 1700s. William Paterson was born in Ireland, immigrated to the United States as a child and rose to prominence, representing New Jersey at the Constitutional Convention and serving as governor and senator for the state. He was also a U.S. Supreme Court justice. His experience, however, was not typical among Irish immigrants. Many came to this country without skills or resources beyond their bodies and were not well educated. They lived in various parts of the area and held different types of jobs; some were domestic servants while others worked on railroads. Many immigrants settled in Newark, which, by 1850, had become an industrial city, a drastic change from its agricultural beginnings. But the overall transition to life in North Jersey was not smooth, and there were often episodes of violence between Protestant "natives" and Catholic newcomers.

Italians

The largest number of immigrants to North Jersey came from Italy, specifically southern Italy. In the mid-1800s, Italy was just emerging as a nation, and immigrants displayed regional pride, continuing to identify with their province even after settling in a new country. They crowded into the cities, primarily Newark, Jersey City, Paterson and Hoboken, which were safer and offered more support for learning English and finding work. They were not readily received by Americans, however. These immigrants were often regarded as intellectually inferior, and they were thought to be prone to radical behavior and criminality; essentially, they were seen as a threat to the "American way." Their supposed radicalism, however, did have some basis in reality. In the late nineteenth century, the city of Paterson was considered a "nest" of Italian anarchism. One immigrant, Gaetano Bresci, left his job and family in the city to return to Milan in 1900, where he shot and killed King Umberto. When Paterson faced labor issues and unrest years later, many were reminded of Bresci's actions, and a stereotype was formed.

The largest waves of Italians came after 1900, and by 1930, the Italian population in New Jersey had reached 191,000. This group was notably one of the more active ethnic groups involved in the labor movement, and many entered local and state politics. Additionally, Italians actively supported the expansion of Catholic churches and institutions across the region.

Jews

Early Jewish immigrants, for the most part, came from German-speaking lands. They established several strong synagogues in the northern part of the state, particularly in Newark, where they congregated. Later immigrants from the eastern parts of Europe spoke other languages and clung to different cultural and religious practices than these early immigrants. This later group was not immediately accepted by the Jews who had already established themselves, but the Jewish schools and hospitals in the area helped the newcomers adapt. Many of the later arrivals brought skills and resources, and many entered into commerce, banking and manufacturing and flourished in the new land. As they prospered, they migrated to suburbs, a trend that accelerated in the 1960s with the racial riots in Newark. But they feared losing their identity as they dispersed, and a strong movement known as MetroWest worked in Essex and Morris Counties to keep them in contact. This effort was largely successful in maintaining their religious—but not ethnic—heritage.

African Americans

Sometimes referred to as "the Georgia of the North," New Jersey was not a friendly place for blacks who were fleeing slavery or racial discrimination in the South. Indeed, slavery was prominent in many areas in New Jersey during colonial times, and there was an active slave market at Perth

Amboy. But slavery died a slow death in the years leading up to the Civil War, and Newark became a primary destination for blacks after the war despite its reputation for poor housing and low-level jobs without potential for improvement. The city's African American population grew from just under 6,700 to nearly 39,000 in three decades. Churches were centers for social and cultural activities, but other organizations, such as the New Jersey Urban League, sprang to life as well. By 1960, there were 330,000 blacks in New Jersey. The highest concentration of blacks was in the older cities (namely Newark), which were being abandoned by whites as they migrated to the suburbs. According to census data, 55 percent of the population in Essex County in 1960 was African American (181,000). The rise in Newark's black population started during the Depression, with numbers rising from 39,000 in 1930 to 70,000 in 1950 and then jumping to 125,000 in 1960 and 220,000 in 1967, just before the riots started. But there was plenty of room, as some 100,000 whites left the city during the 1950s. But still, despite the influx of blacks into the city, Newark lacked adequate housing and jobs, and its local government was largely unsympathetic to the blacks' plight.

Asians

For Asians, the North Jersey experience was different from that of other ethnic groups. In the 1930s, when the national quotas were set blocking further Asian immigration, there were nearly 500,000 Asian immigrants already residing in the United States. Virtually all of these immigrants worked labor-intensive jobs, primarily helping to build railroads and working in the fields. Only a few thousand immigrated to North Jersey. It was not until quotas ended in the 1960s that Asian immigration to the area increased significantly. Although there was a national media trend to identify Asians as a "model minority" because of the contrast with the crime and rioting associated with the black community, many area Asian youths actually became more assertive, inspired by the civil rights movement and also by other events. In the 1980s, the Japanese economic boom contributed to the development of an Asian consciousness and pride that encouraged many young adults to focus on their education and maintain self-discipline so that they would succeed. As with other groups, they were met with a chilly reception and faced discrimination and other obstacles in their pursuit of success.

About one-fifth of New Jersey's Asian population was Chinese. There was also a sizable number of South Asians living in North Jersey, primarily in Edison, Fort Lee and Jersey City. The state soon surpassed Illinois and became the third-largest location for South Asians, behind New York and California. In recent years, many Asians immigrated here seeking professional opportunity, but whereas most ethnic groups emphasized community and family, both husbands and wives worked in Asian families, so family life for this group of immigrants was somewhat different.

OTHER THEMES

The peak immigration years were also years of great disparity between the rich and the poor. A millionaires' row consisting of dozens of mansions sprang up in the Morristown area in the closing decades of the nineteenth century. The crown jewel of these mansions was Florham, built by Hamilton Twombley and his Vanderbilt bride, Florence. The estate was a center of social activity during the few weeks in fall and spring when the couple visited and invited scores of guests to enjoy the scenery and "rustic" atmosphere. There were also other examples of great wealth, such as Lambert Castle in Paterson.

Dutch, German and other north European settlers were scattered across the developing region and assimilated quickly or not according to personal inclinations. Their stories are as varied as the human experience. One tale of interest was the adaptation of Thomas Nast, a nineteenth-century German immigrant who settled in Morristown while working for a New York media company. He became a political cartoonist and created such enduring figures as the Republican elephant and Democratic donkey, as well as "Uncle Sam."

There were many variations on these themes. Some groups were united by their faith and built their activities around their churches, synagogues and mosques. The Jews, the Greeks and the Poles exemplify this trend. Others might share a common language but be divided by their history and circumstance. Ukrainians belonged to Orthodox churches but also to Ukrainian Catholic, Ruthenian Catholic and Ukrainian Protestant churches, and they faced difficulties in finding a common identity in America. The variety of Arab-speaking peoples was quite diverse and consequently confused the locals and stimulated considerable suspicion and

Lambert Castle was a symbol of wealth in Paterson. *Postcard.*

discrimination. This group included Orthodox Christian Palestinians and Lebanese, Arab-speaking Catholics, Muslim groups and Coptic Christians from Egypt. Their lack of comity and frequent quarrels only heightened the difficulties of adaptation to the region.

Despite the difficulties many immigrants shared, they were, overall, pleased that American society offered them a decent education, and many encouraged their children to stay in school, citing such opportunity as a privilege. This factor, in addition to a better standard of living, meant that their children could achieve better lives than their parents. This, of course, was not the case for everyone, but the pattern was prevalent enough that a generalization can be made for these two generations.

The literature of this enormous topic is extensive; the Notes on Sources section at the end of this book is a good place to start exploring more on the subject.

IMMIGRANT INTEGRATION IN NORTH JERSEY

The concentration of immigrants in North Jersey was higher than most other areas in the Northeast (excluding New York City of course), and consequently, North Jersey retains a high level of ethnic diversity. In addition, immigrants experienced a smoother transition into mainstream living compared to many other parts of the country. Public education played the most important role in that transition. Parents who immigrated to North Jersey embraced efforts by teachers to help their children succeed with almost as much zeal as they showed in church. North Jersey has not experienced the latent hostility in recent decades that has produced state restrictions and "English first" initiatives in California and other states. Perhaps it is the diversity of newcomers that has prevented any one particular ethnic image from taking hold in this region. But some long-term trends, such as the rising number of educated immigrants and the high rate of homeownership, suggest that the process of adaptation has been successful. To what extent those trends can be attributed to North Jersey initiatives is open to debate and further study.

On average, some 50,000 people continue to arrive in New Jersey every year, and not all of these newcomers are proficient in English. Integration into society remains an ongoing challenge, one that is largely left to local governments to implement in a way that is consistent with federal law. Immigrant children need educating, and many adults need help learning English as well as establishing themselves. A 2006 study conducted by Fund for New Jersey reported that further efforts to effectively integrate newcomers into New Jersey society were necessary. But this is easier said than done, as the state's growth in recent years is largely attributed to immigrants. According to Charles Stansfield, the influx of 165,000 immigrants between the years 1990 and 1994 did not quite cover the loss of 188,000 Jerseyans who moved out of the state. Some 8,000 in natural population growth made up the difference, creating a small increase in the overall population of the state.

But whereas earlier immigrants shared certain characteristics and goals, namely their quest for employment, more recent waves of immigration show a split that raises a concern. A research study led by William Haller points out that there is a growing divide among second-generation immigrants; those who have a good home life, attend or graduate from decent schools and make an effort to strive for a better life succeed and are often better off than their parents. But without education or stable parenting, they are likely to form or join gangs, do poorly in school and drop out, have trouble finding work above the most menial and low-paying jobs and be burdened early on with the obligations of raising a child. They then fail to improve their lives, and it's likely their children will share the same fate. Some data suggests second- and third-generation immigrants fare no better than the poorest Native Americans, which in turn implies that the American dream is unachievable for many newcomers. It's worth mentioning that failing students are, more and more, considered to be a consequence of poverty rather than a product of inadequate education systems. North Jersey may be among the richest regions in the county, but it shelters significant pockets of poverty that show little sign of disappearing.

THE OTHER HALF

This far into the study, there has been an insufficient treatment of the story of women in North Jersey. There are fewer memoirs and accounts available, which make it more difficult to provide an adequate analysis of their experience as immigrants and citizens. There is enough information, however, to indicate that they faced many difficulties.

Women who immigrated were exposed to various dangers. Many experienced harassment on the voyage over, particularly if traveling in steerage (the lower decks of the ship). Poor housing and health conditions rendered childbearing particularly hazardous, for women as well as their infants. Infant mortality was high in North Jersey well into the twentieth century; Passaic had one of the highest rates of infant mortality in the nation for some years. Employers often refused to hire women who were seeking high-paying jobs, and women were often forced to work the most menial jobs for abominable pay. In 1919, Paterson's silk mills only employed 19 women as skilled spinners. By contrast, Pennsylvania, which had very few silk mills, employed 729 women in such positions.

Some contemporary studies on women's working conditions illustrate the hardships they faced and suggest these are related to the Progressive movement. First, women went to work in manufacturing industries, particularly in textiles. The number of manufacturing establishments in the United States grew by 34 percent between 1904 and 1919, and the number of wage earners grew by 66 percent. In New Jersey, those figures were 58 percent and 91 percent, respectively. The median wage for women in industry was $15.95 per week, and a third worked forty-eight hours or more for that wage. Most of the women were white, and nearly a quarter of them were foreign born. Many of these women were single and lived with their parents or distant relatives. A study of one hundred female workers in Passaic found that many worked at night. (New Jersey was one of the few states that allowed women to work at night and for more than fifty-five hours per week.) Within that group, ninety-six were married and earned between $18 and $20 per week from working night shifts. Their pay supplemented their husbands' income, which was generally $25 to $30 per week per male worker. These women usually slept for only four or five hours a night. According to one study, a family needed to earn between $1,700 and $2,500 a year to get by. The reports by Mary Sayles and Agnes DeLima further examine these issues.

Housing conditions were just as terrible. A study found that many workers lived in five- and six-story buildings, in rooms with a twenty-eight-inch air shaft and few windows. These living quarters were dark, smelly and unhealthy, and there were no regulations landlords had to abide by when leasing rooms. Few places had fire escapes or proper sewage-removal systems. Married women often did piecework at home, making items such as clothing or fireworks. But despite their hardships, women came together and helped each other, and that helped them to survive. According to one account, sixteen young women from Slovakia who were living in a four-room tenement in Passaic took in a newcomer from their home village in the remote Tatra Mountains.

Women's struggle (all women, not just newcomers) to realize their rights and fulfill their destiny was just as difficult and even more prolonged than that of minority groups. Women didn't gain the right to vote until 1920 (though a few women managed to vote, utilizing an oversight in the state's 1776 constitution, which did not specify "all men"), and very few ever held office. The first female was elected to New Jersey's legislature in 1967. By 1993, fourteen women were in the legislature.

Republicans dominated the state assembly from 1873 to the New Deal. Between 1920 and 1946, there were 324 major party candidates vying for a seat on the legislature. Of these 324, 117 were Republicans, and the other 147 were Democrats; 108 women were part of the Republican Party while 36 women were part of the Democratic Party. A few won election in the

The Historic Silk Machinery Exchange, Paterson. *Photo by author.*

Silk workers inside a silk factory in Paterson. *Postcard.*

1920s, but none won a seat on the legislature during the 1930s or '40s. In fact, a study called the years between 1947 and 1965 a time of "expendable women." Only 44 women were elected to public office, and most of these women were Republicans. What's interesting is that 5 were from Bergen County, 19 were from Essex County and 6 were from Hudson County, one of whom was a Democrat. There were 6 from Passaic County, 2 from Morris County and 1 from Union County. In all, 39 were from North Jersey. There were 5 from South Jersey, including 2 from Ocean County and 1 each from the city of Camden, Mercer and Hunterdon Counties. More women would be elected to office in the years after 1965, but to this day, Essex and Bergen Counties have had the most women elected to the legislature of all New Jersey counties.

NORTH JERSEY'S PEOPLE TODAY

New Jersey ranks high regarding the diversity of its population. North Jersey is the reason for that. As with so much else in New Jersey, the exceptional elements are the product of North Jersey; inclusion with the rest of the state waters down that distinctiveness. The table below shows how immigration and socialization illustrates that distinctiveness. The late influx from Asia is actually a national trend; the Asian population in the United States jumped from 480,276 in 2000 to 725,726 in 2010, a 51 percent increase in just ten years' time.

Table A	1910		1960		2000	
N°J Diversity	NJ	N°J	NJ	N°J	NJ	N°J
Total Population (million) (NoJ as percentage of NJ)	2.537	1.772 (70%)	6.067	4.065 (67%)	8.414	4.816 (57%)
Foreign born (million) (percent of total) (percent of state total)	0.660 (26%)	0.549 (31%) (83%)	2.109 (34.8%)	1.610 (39.6%) (76.3%)	1.476 (17.5%)	1.195 (24.8%) (81%)
Asian population (% of state total)			29,800	21,700 (72.9%)	410,000	325,000 (76.3%)

North Jersey is not "counted" as an entity here; these figures are taken from county census statistics for the year 2000. Because the data lumps all Asian nationalities under the descriptor "Asian" and all Hispanics (some of whom are also black) and many ethnic groups under "whites," the figures do not total 100 percent. The data is also dated; significant change has occurred between the year 2000 and 2010. This simplification for reporting minorities suggests there is much less diversity in North Jersey than believed. The 4.916 million people who live in this region were, in 2000, 78.0 percent white, 5.3 percent black and 10.7 percent Asian. Ethnically, Hispanics composed the largest group at 16.0 percent, and Italians constituted the largest nationality group at 15.0 percent.

Significant change took place in the first decade of the new millennium. The white population in North Jersey fell by 112,852, a 3.5 percent drop, while the black population grew by 28,882, a 4.0 percent increase. But the biggest change came in the number of Asians in the area. A whopping 187,637 Asian Americans were living in North Jersey in 2000, a 50.0 percent increase from 1990.

If North Jersey were its own state, it would rank twenty-fifth in the nation for largest population; Bergen County alone would rank higher in population than seven smaller and western states, and it would also outrank them economically. North Jersey would also compete for first in wealth. Eight out of ten of the state's wealthiest communities are in North Jersey, and on average, North Jerseyans who live in these eight communities earn between $70,000 and $86,000 a year; the average per capita income for the whole of North Jersey is $28,086, and the state's is $27,006. But while three of North Jersey's counties (Bergen, Morris and Somerset) are above that last figure, the other five counties are below. The state's core industrial cities in Essex, Hudson and Passaic Counties are still experiencing an influx of immigrants (legal and otherwise) who work as laborers. Immigrants who are well educated and have worked in white-collar professions tend to migrate to the region's more suburban areas rather than the urban centers, as did their predecessors. Considerable gains in the educational achievement of second-generation immigrants, as well as settlement by college-educated immigrants, are noteworthy, both at national and state levels:

EDUCATIONAL ATTAINMENT

Percent Completion		High School	Bachelor's	Advanced Degree
1990	U.S.	75.2	20.3	7.2
	NJ	76.7	24.9	8.8
2000	U.S.	80.4	24.4	8.9
	NJ	82.1	29.8	11.0

Percent Completion				
		High School	Bachelor's	Advanced Degree
2010	U.S.	84.5	27.5	10.1
	NJ	87.0	33.9	12.7

The table shows that the state did not rank exceptionally high or embarrassingly low in terms of education. New Jersey trailed the District of Columbia, Massachusetts, Maryland, New York, Vermont and Virginia. Still, considering the number of newcomers and the challenges they face in acclimating to their new surroundings, New Jersey's accomplishment is remarkable.

The absence of a large city greatly impacted North Jersey. The most populous county, Bergen, ranks fifty-second in the United States for most populated county and comes in behind counties with major cities. Middlesex County ranks sixty-sixth, and Essex ranks seventieth. But when the populations of these three counties are combined, the North Jersey region as a whole is the most densely populated region in the country. And that's something for an area without a huge city. Employment in manufacturing has not disappeared, contrary to popular belief. Middlesex County ranks twenty-ninth in the nation in percent of employment in manufacturing: 9.4 percent of those employed in the county work in manufacturing. Bergen County follows, ranking thirty-first in the nation (9.0 percent), and Essex ranks forty-second (8.3 percent).

A NORTH JERSEY MOSAIC

A study of the eight counties that make up North Jersey reveals some basic realities. The counties can be divided into three categories: central city

(Essex, Hudson and Passaic), later suburban (Bergen, Morris and Somerset) and mixed (Union and Middlesex). Following is a comparison of North Jersey counties with all of the counties in the state. Included are some census comparisons with national averages.

DIVERSITY: Using predominantly non–English speaking households as a gauge for calculating diversity, all eight counties are statistically more diverse than any other region in the United States (an average of 19.6 percent). All but two suburban counties (Morris and Somerset) are more ethnically diverse than the average for the state (at 27.6 percent). Hudson County is the most diverse at (56.0 percent) and Passaic is next highest in the region (44.5 percent). Essex, Union and Middlesex all score higher than 35.0 percent.

POVERTY: Only Passaic County has a higher percentage of poverty (16.5 percent) than the state and the United States as a whole (9.4 percent and 14.3 percent, respectively), according to 2006 data. Obviously, things could have changed by 2012. Four counties have significantly lower rates: Morris (3.8 percent), Somerset (4.4 percent), Bergen (6.6 percent) and Middlesex (7.9 percent). Union County is on par with the state as a whole at 9.5 percent.

OPPORTUNITY: Using the number of minority-owned businesses as the measure for opportunity, we find that there is an exceptionally high percentage of African American–owned businesses in Essex County (21.0 percent). Percentages are also high in Union (13.1 percent), Hudson (11.8 percent) and Passaic (9.5 percent) Counties. The percentage of Hispanic-owned businesses is exceptionally high in Hudson (25.5 percent) and Passaic (17.9 percent) Counties. The percentage of Asian-owned businesses is exceptionally high in Middlesex (19.5 percent) and notably higher than average in Bergen (13.3 percent) and Hudson (12.6 percent) Counties. Only one county can point to the status of its women with pride, and that is Essex County, where 30.9 percent of its businesses are owned by women, which is a little above the state (27.3 percent) and U.S. (28.8 percent) averages. The remainder of the North Jersey counties have relatively low percentages of female-owned business that are either equal to or below state and national averages.

PROSPERITY: White, educated and well off are the three factors (according to data) that confirm many assumptions about the North Jersey region.

While only Morris County has a higher percentage of whites than the average for the United States (82.6 percent versus 72.4 percent), only two suburban counties join it by ranking a higher percentage than the average for the state. The three suburban counties, as well as Middlesex (where Rutgers University is located), have the highest percentage of graduate students with bachelor's degrees or higher: 49.3 percent in Somerset, 48.1 percent in Morris and 44.2 percent in Bergen. The percentage of graduates in Middlesex is 37.4 percent. Somerset and Morris Counties have the highest per capita income, with individuals earning more than $46,000. Bergen is next at $42,174, but only Passaic falls below both the national and state averages at $25,808. Again, the actual figures will be different today, but significant shifts in rankings are not likely. Taken as a whole, North Jersey is financially well off.

CONCLUSION: NEWCOMERS, DIVERSITY AND INNOVATION

This complex topic is best wrapped up with a few general observations. First, the role of newcomers has been critical in the development of North Jersey, but we have only scratched the surface of an enormous topic. Every family's story is unique, as is every experience. A few generalizations can be offered. The first is that there is a tendency to band together and help other immigrants cope with discrimination and the difficulties of adapting to life in a new country. Once these individuals have settled in, the next step is to focus on naturalization, which then leads to ethnic identity rather than immigrant status. Acculturation varies enormously and is strongly influenced by a country's current conditions; local tolerance declined following 9/11. Newcomers who know some English, have prepared themselves, have contacts in place to provide assistance and come from places with strong identities in place have less difficulty adapting.

The road from general labor to the financially comfortable life in North Jersey is not impossible but is certainly difficult. It has been said there are two ways for newcomers to make it here: they can either take the salaried, professional, managerial route that requires a good education or take the entrepreneurial route. Some nationalities favor one route over the other, and typically, Asians tend to succeed in their professional and scholarly pursuits. A memoir by Mitra Kalita reminds us that not everyone who immigrates succeeds nor stays nor necessarily wants to stay. Consider the case of one group of recent newcomers from India who reside around Edison in Middlesex (where some fifty-five thousand compatriots have located). Although this particular family has found employment, bought a house, has children who are doing well at school and is involved in their community, there is no guarantee that any of these things will not change, nor is there a guarantee that they will not experience an upsurge of hostility following a dramatic event like the 9/11 attacks. This particular family is enjoying life in America, but while some feel at home, others still struggle to get comfortable, and some doubt that they ever will.

Part of successful adaptation—and an emerging trend—is the creation of neighborhoods where these immigrants are comfortable. This does not require a "Chinatown"; it typically is a neighborhood where a few families can enjoy a group of others like themselves but are not necessarily a majority. This is particularly noticeable among Asian groups where there are high levels of educational achievement and entry into professional and managerial ranks, especially among the FIRE (finance, insurance and real estate) industries, as well as craft and services industries. Wei Li describes these as "ethnoburbs" and points to the number of neighborhoods in the Southern California region as an example. The description fits neighborhoods in parts of North Jersey as well, namely Morris County, where the author currently resides.

In recent years, immigration has become a major economic factor in global affairs. Large-scale immigration is now commonplace in many parts of the world. An important recent study by Pankej Ghemawat suggests that large-scale, macroeconomic immigration is necessary to avoid cultural decline and macroeconomic imbalances. New migrants still boost the economy without diminishing work for "natives." This analysis offers insight into North Jersey's past and a positive outlook in regard to its continued development in the future. But Ghemawat's theory isn't applicable in many places. For instance, both Queens County, New York, and North Jersey's Hudson County are considered top-ranking "continuous immigration gateways." Both are dynamic communities, but both have high levels of poverty, suggesting that both of these areas aren't experiencing the economic boost Ghemawat argues for. Both counties, however, are accessible to dynamic regions where education opportunities are prominent and creative outlets and startup companies are numerous. The "flows" of people in our global existence appear to be comparable in impact to the flows of capital and information in the health and progress of a region.

CHAPTER 3

"MY WAY":
THE NORTH JERSEY STORY

I traveled each and ev'ry highway
And more, much more than this, I did it my way
—*Frank Sinatra*

Just as North Jersey is not part of New York, it is also not simply part of
New Jersey. It is a distinct place with a unique environment and its own
special set of issues. The goal of this chapter is to find the special North Jersey
story without repeating the well-worn history of the state. Since North Jersey
composes nearly half the state, some state history and background is relevant
and useful in understanding what sets this region apart from the rest of New
Jersey. Understanding North Jersey requires examining and interpreting
events and trends that have shaped those differences. As the story unfolds,
we see several themes that appear, reappear and highlight North Jersey's
distinctiveness. These include divisions and disputes, enterprise and vision,
home rule and innovation in business and public affairs.

It's useful to think of North Jersey's history as a story, for stories have
enormous power and influence, and they are also useful in understanding
individuals as well as groups, organizations and regions. To use a common
phrase, "we are our stories."

DIVISIONS AND DISPUTES

Most of the time, Jerseyans quarrel rather than collaborate. There are so many divisions within New Jersey that one questions what it is that holds the state together. Ignoring the occupancy of the Lenni Lenape, the land was split in two very early, indeed almost simultaneously, with the capture of the region from scattered Dutch settlers in 1664. James Stuart, brother of King Charles II, sent a small fleet to conquer the New Netherlands area. The expedition quickly succeeded, and James designated part of the new territory New Jersey, divided it and gave it to two courtiers, Lord John Berkeley and Sir George Carteret, who became its proprietors. The divided territory had eastern and western halves, which roughly corresponds to the present-day north–south divide. New Jersey then began as two economic enterprises, not one as most states did. Over time, East Jersey morphed into North Jersey. The loss of unity for the Hudson River–New York Harbor estuary enjoyed by the Dutch and its division into two political entities set the stage for economic competition that sometimes fosters but occasionally stifles economic progress.

Agriculture was the economic enterprise of the seventeenth century, and lands were sold and distributed by various means to attract settlers. Upon Carteret's death, a group of twelve investors purchased East Jersey from his widow and reorganized the proprietorship. Over time, the corporation sold most of its lands, but it was not dissolved completely until 1998, when the state purchased the remnants of its holdings.

The Dutch had settled primarily in this east and northern region of this territory, and later colonial immigrants, most of whom were from English-ruled lands, farmed and started various enterprises, selling their goods across the Hudson to markets in New York. This economic tie would only grow stronger over time. Indeed, for many years, royal governors ruled both New York and New Jersey, and it is not surprising that traces of a proprietary attitude endured for a very long time. But whereas the east (north) part of the state quickly became more commercial, the west (south) remained primarily agricultural and retained its landed aristocracy and Anglican influences. It was more reluctant to break away from English rule, and indeed, the large Quaker population that settled in the west helped counterbalance the revolutionary spirit as troubles with England came to a head. Most East Jerseyans, conversely, were more middle-class and Protestant, and the area constantly attracted more immigrants. This area quickly embraced the

New York Harbor. *Postcard.*

Revolution. In the early years of the new nation, Federalists were stronger in the west, while Jeffersonians dominated the east part of the state. Both areas were clearly defined by contrasting political differences, and these differences would play out over the course of the state's history.

Disputes regarding the authority of the proprietors arose when their agents sought to collect taxes (called quitrents) from settlers who were unaccustomed to bearing the expense of their own governance. Quarrels with the assembly at Elizabethtown led to its dismissal in 1668. The issue did not die and underlay renewed disputes when the assembly met again in 1672. British authorities continued to experience difficulties as they attempted to govern the rambunctious colony, and it was during this time that many New Jersey settlers began to consider the benefits of independence.

An early and profound dispute characterizes the time of the American Revolution. A central figure in the story was William Franklin, the obscure—to people outside New Jersey—last royal governor of the colony. Appointed in 1768 with the help of his influential father, Benjamin, Franklin was initially respected by the public since he was a Philadelphia native. He, however, walked into trouble early in his administration when he refused to fire Stephen Skinner, who was suspected of stealing the colony's treasure.

Old Fort, Elizabeth, built 1774. *Postcard.*

Old Snuff Mill, Cedar Grove, Essex County. *Postcard.*

Franklin was finally forced to dismiss Skinner when the new assembly refused to pass legislation for further revenues. Thus, in 1772, a royal governor lost a political struggle with the local assembly, which weakened royal authority before the outbreak of the Revolutionary War.

Actually, the conflict with Franklin was only one in a series. Franklin remained loyal to the Crown and worked to rally Loyalists and disrupt the forces clamoring for a complete break with England. He was arrested in 1776 and held in Connecticut until a prisoner exchange set him free. Franklin worked out of British-controlled New York to recruit spies and others to the Loyalist cause. The struggle between Loyalists and pro-Revolutionary forces in Jersey became so severe that it was described as a civil war. New Jersey, despite being the primary battleground of the conflict, remained deeply divided over the Revolution and provided significant resistance to the Revolutionary cause throughout the struggle. The strategic location led to ongoing campaigns and numerous battles in the area; a current public campaign promotes the region as the "Crossroads of the Revolution." Retribution against Loyalists further embittered relations, particularly between western and eastern sections of the state. The divide between father and son was as definitive as that between rebel and Loyalist. William Franklin joined many Loyalists in living out his later years in England.

After the colonies gained their independence, the state assembly hastily wrote a new constitution in 1776 that included a figurehead governor and powerful legislative assembly. But almost immediately, differences began to reemerge in the state's first national election. There were four candidates from West Jersey and two from East Jersey, and polls in the west were kept open longer until sufficient votes were gathered to elect their slate despite a smaller population. East Jersey quickly turned the tide in the next election, sending their two delegates to Congress.

During the Civil War, many in New Jersey and other parts of the Northeast disapproved of Lincoln and his perceived political agenda. Merchants and manufacturers in Newark, the state's largest city and a substantial port at the time, primarily traded with the South. However, the Civil War threatened to disrupt their trade, and these merchants hoped, at the very least, for a peaceful resolution. Southern New Jersey, meanwhile, primarily supported the South's cause. But the Emancipation Proclamation set off a noisy dissent among residents in both regions, as many felt that Lincoln was no longer trying to preserve the Union but was, instead, trying to end slavery. Many New Jersey recruits, draftees and even entire regiments managed to avoid active conflict, but those who served did so honorably. The state rallied

The Doremus House in Montville was one of many houses in North Jersey that hosted George Washington during the Revolution. *Photo by author.*

Revolutionary-era Tice Tavern, Jersey City. *Postcard.*

around General George McClellan, whom Lincoln had removed from command after the general failed to engage the enemy in several battles, and voted for him in the 1864 presidential race. In 1877, he was elected state governor. This unity, however, proved only temporary, and in the years after the Civil War, divisions and distinctions between the two sides became even more acute.

After the Civil War, the "borders" shifted from east–west to north–south, but the core values of each region remained intact and still endure today. Immigration became an additional factor. The influx of Italian and East European immigrants into the industrialized north half of the state during the latter half of the nineteenth century sharpened the distinctions between the north and south. Many of these immigrants spoke little or no English and were primarily Catholic, whereas New Jersey was largely Protestant. Resentment toward these newcomers led to the "know nothing" movement and establishment of the Native American Party. State Republicans sought to block the enfranchisement of the newcomers with voting restrictions and barriers to the practice of Catholicism. The urban Democrats in northern New Jersey, conversely, worked to quickly enfranchise the newcomers and utilize their votes to ensure their party would have power over local affairs and influence in the state legislature. Suburbanites in Bergen County and elsewhere sometimes took on anti-urban attitudes as well. On occasion, the state assembly moved to take over city police, fire or utility departments to replace the elected newcomer-dominated administrations with people more to their liking (generally white Protestants). With one senator and at least one House member from each county, the growing and diverse city received little sympathy or attention from state officials in Trenton. The only exception to this lack of attention was the governor's office, which was the only public office elected directly by the people. Consequently, most of New Jersey's governors elected during the nineteenth century were Democrats.

The growing ethnic diversity was a factor in a unique fragmentation of local governance that has complicated the governance of New Jersey. Between 1861 and 1930, New Jersey restructured itself from about one hundred large municipalities into more than six hundred municipalities that range in size from cities to burgs the size of golf courses with fewer than twenty residents. These divisions emerged as people argued over such issues as:

• Wet versus dry: some wanted to prohibit alcohol sales on Sundays.
• Schools: many communities quarreled over policies and attitudes.

- Roads: town dwellers wanted paved streets while those who lived in rural areas wanted minimum road maintenance.
- Revenues: communities competed over the control of mines and rail junctions or sought to separate from concentrations of new and different immigrants.

Most of these new municipalities are concentrated in North Jersey, and they continue to cause a number of political, economic and social problems. The cost of more than six hundred school superintendents and hundreds of civil servants and managers has created unsustainable debt and pension obligations that were exacerbated by the 2008 recession. Prospects for solving the problem are dim, as Alan Karcher, former state assembly speaker, explains: "Jerseyans are happy to change their constitution almost annually but the municipal borders are seemingly cemented in place for decades under the flag of a phantom 'home rule legacy.'"

VISION AND INNOVATION

New York overshadows North Jersey as a remarkably innovative region. Vision is the imagining or perceiving of something that does not exist but can be created. Oftentimes, it is considered a trait of a successful leader. Innovation, meanwhile, is something new that enables change and the improvement of a process, product or situation, and it, too, relates to leadership. To suggest that North Jersey is characterized by vision and innovation is to assert that the area has produced leaders and innovators in significant aspects of life and culture. And, on this point, the evidence is clear.

Innovation emerged in North Jersey in waves. Colonel John Stevens, the inventor of the steamboat, was part of the first wave. Born to a prominent New Jersey family, he served as a captain in Washington's army and later as treasurer of the state. His steamship efforts were preceded by the work of John Fitch, who built a working steamship in 1786, and by Robert Fulton, who used New York connections to close the Hudson River to Stevens, forcing Stevens to send his best vessel to Philadelphia to work the Delaware River traffic. But Stevens's real ambition was to put his steam engine to work on land and demonstrate its usefulness and potential. He is considered the founder of the railroad industry. His sons carried on his work, gaining the first charter and establishing the enormously successful Camden & Amboy Railroad. Another visionary whose achievement had a great impact on North Jersey was George P. McCulloch, an engineer and teacher from Morristown. Fascinated by the progress of the Erie Canal in New York, he envisioned connecting the Delaware and Hudson Rivers to ease the transport of coal to the iron industries in and around Newark. This commitment led to the creation of the Morris Canal, which still stands as a great engineering achievement as it cuts through the mountains; it also had a significant impact on North Jersey's economy in its day.

Newark was the scene of wide-ranging experiments and industrial breakthroughs in the early nineteenth century. What we now understand as clustering developed around such industries as leather goods, jewelry and metalworks. Inventor Seth Boyden made a number of large breakthroughs, from perfecting patent leather to a nail-making machine. An influx of immigrants from Ireland and Germany fueled the city's industrial output, and between the years 1826 and 1860, Newark doubled and redoubled in size, growing from 8,000 people to 72,000. Chemistry professor James Jay Mapes established an early experimental farm where he tested fertilizers and other agricultural improvements.

Shipyards were constructed in Jersey City and produced the steamships of Robert Fulton's enterprise. Porcelain and brick manufacturing were two of the city's other big industries. In the 1820s, William Colgate moved his soap factory to Jersey City and built an enormously successful business. Just a few miles north, Paterson revived and realized Alexander Hamilton's vision of an industrial city. The Colt family produced some of the weapons that "won the West," and Thomas Rogers began a locomotive manufacturing enterprise that—augmented by other manufacturers—turned out the engines that allowed the Union to subdue the South and provide much of the power to forge the vast lands of the western frontier into a nation. Textiles, and later the silk industry, expanded to include many producers and drew thousands of immigrants to labor on their looms.

As substantial as this work was, it pales in comparison to what followed in the "neighborhood" in the last half of the century. There, the colossal figure is Thomas Edison, the creator of entirely new industries that ushered in what we think of as the modern age. The prototypical inventor was more a tinkerer than visionary, and many of the products that came out of his 1,300 patents actually were actually used in other ways than his original intents. For our purposes, it was his creation of the "invention factory" at

The famous and huge Colgate Clock (left) at the Jersey City waterfront. *Postcard.*

Restored Rogers locomotive, Paterson Museum. *Photo by author.*

The lab, offices and machine shop of Edison in Menlo Park were not luxurious but were historically productive and entrepreneurial. *Postcard, Edison Museum. Photo by author.*

Menlo Park, later moved to West Orange in Essex County, that is his most important achievement.

Edison did not work in isolation; he hired engineers and inventors to help him realize his goals, and he interacted with others who were also making major breakthroughs. Edward Weston invented the electric dynamo and moved his operation to Newark since that was "where the action was." John Wesley Hyatt synthesized celluloid and began producing products like billiard balls; he moved his enterprise to Newark in 1873. Celluloid was the breakthrough that led to the development of the plastics industry; many spinoff industries followed. Irish immigrant John P. Holland refined his plans for a submarine while teaching in Paterson and ran his first successful test in the Passaic River. He eventually gained contracts and built the first operational submarines for the U.S. Navy. Later the British, Japanese and others utilized his plans to build their models. Additional sites of innovation in this area include the village of Roselle in Union County, which is where Edison's first electric plant was located, and it was also the first town with electric streetlights. And Robert Woods Johnson and his brother had a factory in nearby New Brunswick that produced antiseptics to reduce infections and make surgery much less hazardous. Johnson and Johnson became one of the most respected healthcare companies in the world.

The surge of innovation was stimulated by another form of immigration. Ambitious men relocated to North Jersey to benefit from the high level of innovation and experimentation already underway. Such immigrants (mostly from other states in the United States) included Edison, Colgate, Hyatt, Holland and Weston. The process was an early rendition of what we now refer to as economic clustering.

INDUSTRIAL RESEARCH

The idea of the research lab flowered in North Jersey in the twentieth century. Chemical and medical companies in particular developed labs in what we know as pharmaceuticals, an industry of enormous size and social impact. The industry is dynamic and competitive, with many mergers and acquisitions, but many labs and some headquarters remain in New Jersey. The primary breakthroughs included the development of sulfas (Squibb) and the mass production of penicillin (Merck scientists). Merck also developed vitamin B1, which initiated a huge vitamin industry grounded in the region. North Jersey labs were also the sites for early development of several tranquilizers. Pharmaceuticals became a cluster phenomenon in mid-twentieth-century North Jersey.

The new phenomenon was something far more than Edison's Menlo Park. One of the premier research laboratories of the age, Bell Labs, enjoyed its most impressive home and structure at the Murray Hill facility in New Providence–Berkeley Heights. But the start of formal industrial research actually occurred elsewhere, in the efforts of General Electric (mostly in Manhattan) and Bell (a subsidiary of AT&T), primarily in Boston). The organization and process of industrial research involved creating facilities; hiring new science PhDs; and putting together teams of scientists, engineers, mathematicians and technicians to work on special projects or (later) original research. The focus was on practical applications to support new products or the improvement of existing products in order to gain competitive advantage. The application and utilization of patents symbolized the pace and scale of productivity of the research, and both companies benefitted greatly from the investments and effort. Bell Labs would spin off numerous plants and centers all across Greater North Jersey.

In the 1960s, North Jersey produced more than half of the chemicals used in the United States. From its first refinery in Bayonne, the region became the locus of major petrochemical research, such as that at the Esso Research center in Linden (Union County). This work spills over into plastics, where major developments included vinyl, polyethylene and various resins. Petrochemical experimentation and development also led to synthetic rubber research centered in Wayne in Passaic County. The story goes on and on. By the mid-1960s, important contributions had been made and reported on solid-state technology, explosives and rocket propulsion. The development of major improvements in paints made the region the heart of that industry. Additional chapters of the story clustered around Bell Labs and their work in telecommunications, semiconductors and information theory.

The question for us is why. Several explanations are available. First is the impact of the research lab and a fundamental change in the research process itself. In the twentieth century, research became complex and increasingly multidisciplinary. No one person can have enough expertise in numerous fields to achieve the breakthroughs and move from discovery to innovation to production. Usually, many scientists, engineers and lab technicians are involved in major research projects—enterprises far larger than even Thomas Edison could assemble. Moving from theory to product involves many more people and additional expertise. Clusters form around such research activity to support existing enterprise, as Michael Gibbons and colleagues make clear. And Richard Florida (2002) points out that exciting research and creativity attract additional researchers and "creatives."

Having the financial resources of New York and intellectual resources of two major accessible universities (Princeton and Rutgers) were important factors. The concurrent rise of corporatism, with its typical massive accumulation of financial resources, made such expensive enterprises and payrolls feasible. New Jersey's pro-business reputation and its adoption of lax rules for incorporation were important attractions. Location and transportation certainly played a role as well, as did the presence of corporate offices and headquarters in the region and nearby New York. But many elements of this phenomenon were indigenous to the region, and New York benefitted from it as much or more than its contribution to this clustered and dynamic process.

Finally, it must be noted that the process is one of research and development, discovery and implementation. This was not about basic research but about important research that was needed and approved by society as a whole. To bring this down to practical reality, we note the research showing a link between contextual knowledge spillover (within a given field) and innovation leading to geographic concentration. Greater concentration produces higher returns and greater economic development. The small size of North Jersey means that research and development can more easily spill over between disciplines; the concentration of labs and research efforts feeds upon itself and makes the area competitive with California, Massachusetts and New York.

There is another level of work to consider. For every Edison, Stevens or Einstein, there will be dozens of such researchers/scholars/administrators who were productive. John R. Pierce is one such example. He took a position at Bell Labs in 1936 after earning a PhD from Cal Tech and put in thirty-five years at the facility while raising a family and maintaining a home in nearby Berkeley Heights. He led the team that developed the transistor (which he named). Working with many outstanding people (including Claude Shannon, with whom he developed pulse code modulation), he later led the division that developed communications satellites, starting with Telstar. He authored several technical books on information and communications technologies and also wrote science fiction under the pen name J.J. Coupling. He was not a "native" of North Jersey, but he found it to be a good place to do productive work. Pierce observed that one of the great things about Bell Labs was that when the project at hand played out or proved unpromising, a researcher could easily switch to something else, which was very difficult to do when government funding was involved.

Such innovation does not necessarily continue indefinitely. A 2005 follow-up study by the New Jersey Technology Council found that while there were still important centers of technology innovation in the state, there were alarm bells sounding, including a slowing of business startups, falling patent productivity, declining investment in research and development and a shortage of scientists and engineers. The state has provided substantial support for this work, but analysis uncovered significant abuse and waste. Nevertheless, business and corporate innovation is one of the more distinctive characteristics of North Jersey's economic and social development.

HOME RULE

One of the cornerstones on which North Jersey's distinctive culture and innovative spirit are founded is the political belief in home rule. The concept can be traced back to colonial times, when many resisted the proprietary's and royal government's efforts to tax the colony. Additionally, colonists had to provide their own schools, roads and meeting places if they were to have any such public facilities. That independent spirit endured even after the new nation was formed. Short on money and hampered in commercial and enterprise development by their two larger neighboring states, government-paid services came slowly, if at all. But by 1798, the state began to recognize existing township structures. The state's 1776 constitution endorsed home rule, essentially allowing people to govern themselves in their communities without interference from the state. This was confirmed by the 1947 constitution, which allowed people to break away from existing communities and establish their own (which caused the aforementioned division of large municipalities into smaller ones). Over the years, various political structures were recognized: townships became boroughs, boroughs became towns and towns became cities. Economic initiatives were most often certified through local charters, such as those granting monopolies for canals and railroads, and these cost the taxpayers nothing and generated enough revenue to cover the required taxes.

Home rule still plays a major part in New Jersey's political process. For example, the state legislature passed a law in 1955 forbidding unfunded mandates to the towns by the state. But despite being a provision of the state constitution, home rule isn't easily put into practice. The rapid urbanization that accompanied the Industrial Revolution led to state initiatives and laws that have, step by step, limited the realities of home rule. Modern society requires safety and security measures, including codes for building construction, certification of financial officers, law enforcement and so forth. As a result, the power of the state has steadily increased over the years, and it has become more and more involved with municipal affairs.

This all revolves around the question of whether municipalities are creatures of the state and subject to their rule or whether they preceded the state and therefore had traditional and historic rights. Probably no topic has provided greater grounds for contention on this issue than the operation of the public schools, which have generally been left in the hands of the municipalities. But the education divide—a consequence of the disparity between suburban education and inner-city education—created many inequalities, and in 1990, the state finally realized something had to be done. In the landmark case *Abbott v. Burke*, the New Jersey Supreme Court required the state to enact legislation that allowed for equal funding of urban and suburban school districts. Governor Jim Florio pushed the Quality Education Act, which assured equal expenditures for all schoolchildren regardless of the level of local support, through the state legislature, as well as a tax bill to help fund the schools. There was an extreme negative reaction among voters, and Florio was not reelected in 1994, losing to Christine Todd Whitman.

The underlying issue of local control and state responsibility for equal protection continues to roil the waters of New Jersey politics. This particular issue is not strictly a North Jersey issue but rather a divisive one within the region that affects school systems in the old industrial centers of Jersey City, Newark and Paterson and the suburban and exurban areas where residents are already burdened with high taxes but enjoy excellent public schools. The state had to take control of the schools for all three cities in question, and all received large additional revenues for years to equalize the educational effort. While two of the cities have shown adequate improvement to regain some control over their school operations, Paterson has not shown sufficient progress and remains under state supervision. The matter remains a divisive matter and is only heightened by the recent recession and the confrontational politics of Governor Chris Christie. The limitations of home rule legality stand to complicate politics for some time to come.

Other North Jersey–South Jersey differences exist as well. In North Jersey, any real estate closing requires that the parties be represented by counsel. For years, the practice in South Jersey was that the role of title companies made such representation unnecessary. This became an issue, however, and was taken to the state supreme court in 1993. The court ruled that while representation by counsel was preferred and recommended, South Jersey's use of title companies was an established practice in the region and had been for a number of years. The court then declined to force the region to change.

So if essential issues like educational opportunity cannot be managed on the local level to satisfy the state, is there a need for an intermediate political or governing body? Should there be a regional level of government to help provide political solutions for municipalities troubled by state intervention in their affairs? These are questions for future consideration.

INNOVATION IN PUBLIC AFFAIRS

Because it is smaller, older and strategically located near the nation's commercial and cultural hub, New Jersey had to deal with new issues and developments earlier than most states. And North Jersey was typically where things came together more visibly and urgently than elsewhere. We have seen how vision and innovation characterized the area's economic development, so it is reasonable to expect innovation in other areas of life as well. In the case of governance and public affairs, this expectation is fulfilled, though more often by faceless public servants and commissions than by highly visible entrepreneurs.

North Jersey has repeatedly been the scene of public affairs initiatives. And just as John Stevens revolutionized land transportation, so did others foresee adaptations, like traffic circles and superhighways, to make the system more effective. The New Jersey Turnpike served as a model for the national Interstate Highway System that brought the nation closer together in the 1960s and in the years that followed. The amount of land paved over by highways covered a significant portion of North Jersey. It is no wonder then that the region addressed the issue of land-use planning and zoning so early in its history. The result was zoning ordinances, tax code incentives and disincentives and planning for roads and other public infrastructure, such as water supply, sewage management and utilities

Planning and zoning in particular is a category where home rule has been eclipsed in part to meet greater needs. Two simultaneous events illustrate how regional planning—with local collaboration—affected change.

In 1969, the Meadowlands Commission was created with the mission of bringing order to a thirty-one-square-mile wetland area in the delta of the Hackensack and Passaic Rivers, which was the site of intense interest from developers. The establishment of rail lines after 1830 disrupted the area's ecology, as did the construction of the overpass in 1950. Over the years, the wetland has been characterized as a toxic dump, a mob burial ground and a rich wildlife preserve. Indeed, it was all of these things.

Highway construction disrupted Bergen County's landscape. *William F. Augustine Photo Collection, Special Collections, Alexander Library, Rutgers University.*

The commission's work involves fourteen municipalities in Bergen and Hudson Counties and has two seemingly contradictory tasks: control the economic development of the lands while protecting as much of the natural habitat as possible. The work involves endless negotiation and mediation, and oftentimes, neither developers nor environmentalists are satisfied. Development is still happening, but the commission's efforts to utilize such principles as "no net loss" of wetlands and restoration are allowing the marshlands to continue and even thrive in several locales. The commission had some success, and it has a commendable record of balancing two seemingly irreconcilable forces in that it oversees dynamic commercial and business growth while preserving places of historic and natural beauty.

A different outcome resulted from a plan by the New York Port Authority to build an additional airport in Morris County on four thousand acres of natural wetlands known as the Great Swamp. The proposed jetport would extend far beyond the wetlands and force the removal of more than seventy families from their homes. When the plan was made public in early

December 1959, a number of citizens and organizations—concerned about the inevitable increase of traffic and noise, damage to water supplies and disruption of property values and tax revenues—responded almost immediately. The ensuing struggle proved to be an important lesson on the power of community organization and citizen action against politically savvy professionals vying for progress. Some six thousand individuals and 496 organizations rallied support and donations from around the country and successfully blocked the project. In 1964, a federal "wildlife refuge" law was passed, and four years later, President Lyndon Johnson signed the law, creating the Great Swamp Wildlife Refuge, a unique local attraction.

In regard to environmental issues, New Jersey has had its successes and its failures. The state passed the nation's first air pollution–control law in 1954, but when the federal superfund was created to clean up toxic waste sites in 1982, the state ranked first in number of toxic sites. That should not come as a surprise, given the level of scientific research and industrial experimentation previously mentioned. What is alarming is that while New Jersey was allocated nearly half the superfund monies between 1980 and 1988, only 23 sites were completed by 2005, and 113 remained in need of cleanup. On the positive side, the amount of toxic waste produced by the state had decreased by 75 percent by 1997.

The latest, most difficult and most disputed of the state's land-use efforts is the Highlands Water Preservation and Planning Act, which was signed into law by Governor James McGreevey in 2004. The act impacted dozens of municipalities in seven counties in the northwestern part of the state (our Greater North Jersey), and it aimed to provide water, preserve wildlife and curb development. However, it has not been adequately funded, and the plan fails to satisfy environmentalists, builders and farmers, the latter of whom stood to enjoy profits from selling land to developers. The vision was awesome, but implementing the plan will be a bone of political contention for years to come.

Conclusion

One of the strengths of American government is the states' ability to innovate. Failures are more manageable at this level than the federal level, and good ideas can be easily adopted and applied to other states or even on the national level. Likewise, the home rule in New Jersey allows communities to handle problems in their own way—to be innovative—and this is, again, a chief trait of North Jersey communities.

Of course, not all initiatives discussed in this chapter were indigenous to North Jersey. North Jersey does not exist in isolation: it is a thoroughfare for a very large megalopolis that is a primary engine for the development of a powerful and dynamic nation. As outlined at the beginning of the book, North Jersey interacts with and is greatly influenced by New York, as well as other parts of the country and the world. What has happened in North Jersey is only sometimes unique and innovative but sufficiently so that the region must be viewed as a place of vision and innovation. Land-use policy is not unique to North Jersey, but certainly, many initiatives were generated here that served and continue to serve as a model for others. Additionally, many of the scientific and technical innovations were made in corporate labs by teams of highly skilled people from around the country. While the innovators lived in North Jersey during their creative gestation, not all of them stayed. But this illustrates how North Jersey works with outside influences and creates partnerships and helps us to understand the role North Jersey has played in the development of modern America. Foresight to join with others to accomplish something that cannot be accomplished alone is one characteristic of leadership; North Jersey has exemplified that character trait. Doing it "my way" does not necessarily mean doing it alone.

CHAPTER 4

SUBURBS OR WHAT?

Cities are an immense laboratory of trial and error, failure and success, in city building and city design.
—Jane Jacobs

Cities have played a major role in the human experience for thousands of years. The city is a process, not an event. It is the product of a village's political power, according to Lewis Mumford, or in some cases, economic power, according to Jane Jacobs. As it develops, so does the region around it. But these regions can be cleared, transformed, bypassed or abandoned. The larger number of people requires organization and leads to bureaucracy, transportation, communication and expansion. The process is now outdated. It was once thought that the city would be absorbed into what is called a megalopolis in the final stage of urbanization. But something else happened instead, both in North Jersey and elsewhere.

NORTH JERSEY'S CITIES

North Jersey's cities have followed, for the most part, the usual pattern of growth that occurs during periods of industrialization. Four of its cities' populations grew to more than 100,000 between the 1860s and 1920s.

Newark, 1908. *Postcard.*

Newark's population reached 105,000 by 1870 and grew to 437,000 by 1950. It declined slightly after 1960 and dropped significantly following the 1967 riots. In 2000, its population was 273,500, but that number has steadily increased since 2010.

Jersey City's population reached 100,000 in the mid-1870s and fluctuated from decade to decade. The population peaked in 1930 at 316,000 and has since declined. The city's population in 2010 was 250,000. In the mid-1920s, Elizabeth's population increased to 100,000, and it continued to grow, only dropping occasionally. The population in 2010 was 125,000.

These three cities surrounding Newark Bay compose a single urban complex, to which can be added Bayonne and Kearney. The combined population of these five municipalities reached almost a million (978,489) in 1950 and then declined by 22 percent (762,735) by 2010. One wonders what advantages there may be in greater collaboration between these cities.

Although not a part of this Newark Bay area, Paterson (which is in Passaic County) is one of the four cities that experienced a population boom. By 1900, the population had increased to 105,000, but in the years that followed, growth was slight. By 2000, the population had reached 149,000 but then started to decline.

Broad Street in downtown Elizabeth, early twentieth century. *Postcard.*

Downtown industrial Paterson, early twentieth century. *Postcard.*

By the middle of the twentieth century, all of North Jersey's cities had begun to decline. City functions, such as providing necessities such as schools, public services and facilitating acculturation, had lost their force. Additionally, second- and third-generation immigrants, driven by ambition, joined the exodus and relocated a few miles farther from these urban centers. Usually, cities lose their edge as engines of economic development and begin to resort to what Jane Jacobs describes as "transactions of decline," such as subsidies and welfare. North Jersey cities followed this pattern.

SUBURBANIZATION

The escape from the city to a more pastoral, relaxed, upscale lifestyle a bit farther away has enjoyed a "serial enchantment" for Americans through much of our history. There have been repeated surges of movement. The first of several waves of suburbanization began early in the nineteenth century (the 1820s and 1830s), as the well-to-do moved to "borderlands" to escape city crowding. In the middle decades of the century, light rail made it easier for the wealthy to move a bit farther into picturesque enclaves with more privacy. Characteristics of these enclaves included freestanding homes with yards along tree-lined streets. These developments were limited in scale and did not greatly impact larger social patterns to this point. Streetcar-oriented buildouts emerged in the last third of the century. A common characteristic was a widespread longing to live closer to nature, in sight of trees and hills. Between 1880 and the 1930s, thousands of articles in such magazines as *Country Life* lauded the escape from the city. The desire to have a "landscape" view has been compared to the traditional American urge to "go West" and settle the frontier.

The shift from cities to suburbia is experienced in most advanced societies, particularly those with an automobile culture (which is most places). Characteristics of modern suburbia include reliance on the automobile, upward mobility, nuclear families, conspicuous consumption and social separateness, even exclusion. The automobile allows people to live farther from work in freestanding homes on large lots amid general affluence.

A suburb in Elizabeth, early twentieth century. *Postcard.*

As elsewhere in America, suburbanization in North Jersey peaked in the 1950s and 1960s. Emerging towns—Wayne in Passaic County, Morris Township in Morris County and Springfield Township in Union County, to name a few—more than doubled in size in just ten years. Some of these places leveled off or even declined slightly in the next decade, but those with appeal continued to grow. Morris, Hunterdon and Monmouth Counties all nearly tripled in population between 1950 and 2000. But this takes us outside our territory.

One interesting explanation for the suburbanization trend was the general attitudes of returning World War II veterans. Many of them witnessed the devastation of carpet bombing and firebombing in Germany while others played a part in the devastation of Hiroshima or Nagasaki. On returning to the flimsy apartment buildings and row houses in which they lived, many decided to seek sturdier homes that were surrounded by more space. All across the United States, people made their way to the suburbs, North Jerseyans included.

This demographic transformation was also a result of change in the methods and means of shopping. Communities that are built around large cities often develop downtown shopping districts, and small stores serve the basic needs of the local community. But large highways and shopping malls disrupt that pattern. In 1957, two groundbreaking malls—Bergen

Mall and Garden State Mall—opened almost simultaneously in Bergen County about a mile apart, and each featured approximately one million square feet of space, extensive parking, a few department store anchors and up to one hundred additional shops. The shopping malls disrupted small and downtown areas all around the county, and their presence was even felt in New York. Historically, the expanding freeway system facilitated access to malls, which resulted in the disruption of the existing purchasing patterns. The process kept accelerating, and by the end of the century, there were a dozen large malls in North Jersey, as well as additional centers throughout the state.

Essentially, all this economic growth without regional planning created a mess. Communities faded into memory while urban sprawl split neighborhoods and made them more a product of accident than intent. One solution proposed by city officials across the nation was to revive residential areas by constructing walkways and bike paths, permanent green preserves and traffic corridors and to provision for undesirable facilities such as power plants, affordable housing and garbage dumps. Many planners and urbanists agreed, but carrying out the plan proved problematic.

In fairness, there have been repeated efforts to design a plan to create logical and livable cities. In the 1920s, urban planners in New York City discussed establishing "regional cities," but none was ever established. Out of the number of plans, two were in North Jersey: Radburn and Hackensack Meadows. The Radburn vision was a satellite city that would, in theory, further the decentralization of the central city. It would produce a town of three thousand residents and feature auto-free central spaces to allow more residences in less space while keeping highways at arm's length with super blocks and concentrated parking. The model, however, revealed flaws and was not developed beyond an initial plot. The Hackensack Meadows site sought to reduce congestion with planned areas for industry, commerce and residences. That area has turned into a hub of highways and office buildings around a huge sports complex.

Suburbanization is a common subject of literature on New Jersey. In *New Jersey Politics and Government*, authors Barbara and Stephen Salmore characterize the state as suburban, but this is misleading; there is no city for the area to encircle and support. Sometimes the entire region is considered urban, but that is misleading as well. There are areas of land throughout the state that remain essentially rural, with woodlands, farms

Mansions reflecting the "good life" in North Jersey. *Photo by author.*

and scattered residences. Additional work is needed in the way of theory and description.

There is another dimension to the North Jersey suburb: the suburb itself has become a symbol of affluence and upper-class living. This shift occurred as prosperous groups, such as doctors, investment bankers and corporate officers, sought more exclusive neighborhoods in the waning years of the twentieth century. Oftentimes, builders reserved entire sections of land for spacious homes to meet the desire for expansive homes on large lots in hilly terrain amidst environmentalist efforts to preserve woodlands. Montville serves as an excellent example. A mile south from Towaco Station, there is an area of $1 million mansions, each featuring a unique architectural design, three-car garage and elaborate landscaping.

Although North Jersey experienced the suburban phenomenon, it lacks a major city. In fact, there is no real city in all of New Jersey. There is also no major television station or professional football or baseball team. For some, those were provided by New York, but these people are in the minority. Meanwhile, more and more New Yorkers are commuting to work in North Jersey. Why is that so? And what does it all mean? One explanation can be found in examining the concept of the edge city.

EDGE CITIES

A best-selling book with a new idea can impact public perception. Joel Garreau's *Edge City* illustrates this nicely. He makes the case that in the last quarter of the twentieth century, a new type of city emerged to meet the social and economic needs at a time when services and knowledge were more economically important than production and when a new world of airports, freeways and satellite communication freed individuals from living and working in suburbs and urban centers. In the first chapter of this book, Garreau discusses how this is important for New Jersey, which he calls "tomorrowland." He identifies ten edge cities in the state, eight of which are in North Jersey: Bridgewater, Fort Lee, Meadowlands-Hoboken, Mahwah, Metropark, Paramus-Montvale and Woodbridge. The other two are in Central and South Jersey (Princeton and Cherry Hill, respectively). But what does that mean for our story?

Garreau defines an edge city as a relatively new area with a minimum of five million square feet of office space (the workplace of the Information Age); six thousand square feet of leasable retail space (a large shopping mall will do); and more jobs than bedrooms. Edge cities appear in locales where little existed forty years earlier and are sometimes called technoburbs, suburban centers or perimeter cities. Few of them, however, have sidewalks, and most have little public space. Additionally, they are dispersed across boundaries, so none has a municipal government or a mayor. The convergence of the automobile, superhighways, air travel and the computer made the edge city possible.

According to Garreau, edge cities qualify as cities in that they provide jobs, entertainment and commerce, which are all traditionally provided by a city, only these new cities lack skyscrapers. They are closer to where people live, which makes it easier to commute, and they are generally safer than large urban centers. The quality of life holds great appeal; a family can live in a large home on a large lot for the same amount of money one would spend on a small apartment in Manhattan.

Garreau may have popularized the idea, but others were developing additional explanations for the phenomenon. Sometime in the mid-twentieth century, manufacturing and commerce shifted from the city to other areas. The new arrangement was spatially dispersed. Whereas a major city like New York, Berlin or London might cover one hundred square miles, the new edge city might spread across more than two thousand square miles, with villages, forestlands, factories and other enterprises sitting under a virtual, invisible, perhaps nonexistent umbrella of an assumed organization. Highway networks, a new mortgage system favoring single-family dwellings and the rise of two-income families—as more and more women chose or were compelled to pursue careers—contributed to the creation of these "cities."

This was a separate phenomenon from the corporate "exodus" from the city, which was a decisive trend that peaked in the 1970s. Connecticut benefitted first from this trend, then parts of North Jersey, notably Morris and Somerset Counties. Some of the office space surely counted in Garreau's edge city figures, but these facilities were spread out over a large area and driven by their own unique standards. Social critic William H. Whyte realized something was happening when he observed the towers of Las Colinas grouped outside Dallas. He perceived how this facility signaled a new importance of the combination of highway interchanges, airports, shopping malls and large hotels with conference facilities. Like Garreau, Whyte saw the New (North) Jersey experience as the most spectacular example. Its growth, however, came at the expense not of New York but of the older urban centers in North Jersey where, as we have seen, population declined in the middle decades of the twentieth century.

The new reality came with notable costs. Sense of community was one casualty, as was diversity. There was nothing to root identity, and some places often didn't even have names. But there was substance to the phenomenon, as the following chart illustrates.

NORTH JERSEY POPULATION SHARE BY REGION

Year	Core Counties*	Suburb±	Total North Jersey	Outliers	Greater North Jersey	South Jersey
1850	33%	16%	49%	27%	76%	24%
1900	57%	9.4%	67%	15%	81%	19%
1950	59%	10.9%	70%	12%	82%	18%
2000	39%	18%	57%	19%	77%	23%

* The five counties of Gale's Greater New Jersey
± Includes Middlesex, Morris and Somerset Counties

The outliers column denotes counties to the west of North Jersey (Hunterdon, Sussex and Warren), plus Mercer and Monmouth. All together, these thirteen counties make up Greater North Jersey.

Out of all the groups, the core North Jersey region developed the most during the late nineteenth and early twentieth centuries. That growth slowed after 1950 in comparison with the suburban region, the outliers and even South Jersey.

Edison and Woodbridge's population growth reflects some of the suburban or post-urban edge city phenomenon rather than following the traditional pattern of city growth. Neither is dispersed, containing only thirty or twenty-four square miles of territory, respectively. Edison's present boundaries were set around 1950, and the city was formally organized and named in 1954. Woodbridge Township was an early settlement that dates back to the seventeenth century. Portions of it have separated and become part of either Edison or Rahway. It is much more of a suburb than a city.

Looking at the first row on the chart, the various regions of the state were fairly balanced, which suggests the economy across the state was primarily agricultural. In the last half of the twentieth century, people migrated into suburban and edge regions that were growing in popularity at a time when commuting was commonplace and when commercial and industrial businesses were looking to expand outside the city.

The figures also suggest that North Jersey may have danced to its own tune rather than to that of New York. The region went through its own stages of development, moving from agriculture to industry to services and information. Not even the core regions' development can be explained as an adjunct to New York. It seems then that New York's influence did not determine the process or the outcome that is present-day North Jersey. So, then, what was decisive? And where do we go from here?

REGIONAL ISSUES

The edge city phenomenon, to the extent it occurred, can also be seen in a larger, regional context of innovations in transportation, production and institution building. North Jersey was a center, perhaps the critical hub, of this process. Why is this so? Were there some enormous challenges to overcome? What led to the wealth, dynamism and productivity of this region?

Early nineteenth-century roads—called turnpikes at the time—canals and then railroads were mainly built by private investors. The location of North Jersey on the corridor between New York and Philadelphia, Boston and the South was critical even in colonial times. Postmaster Ben Franklin spent much time in New Jersey establishing the offices and links of the colonial postal system. The North Jersey area was a critical battleground for the American Revolution, and General George Washington wintered in Morristown twice in conditions as difficult as the legendary camp at Valley Forge. The area is strategically critical.

But location does not guarantee accomplishment. Something else has to occur. Business and private investors built the roads, canals and railroads that lead across New Jersey to the docks and warehouses of Newark and other waterfronts on the lower Hudson River. But the massive river also proved to be a barrier. The number of ferries and barges doubled and then redoubled but could not keep up with the demand for crossing. This remained a problem until the twentieth century, and for a time the will and expertise to cross the barrier remained inadequate to the task.

Some of the challenges faced then are dealt with by institutions today. The Regional Plan Association, which is headquartered in New York and

The steps down from the Palisades to the Hudson River, Weehawken, 1908. *Postcard.*

Lackawanna Station, Newark. *Postcard.*

The Hamburg-American pier, Hoboken. Seagoing ships docked on North Jersey's Hudson shore.

Princeton, is promoting fast rail lines and producing excellent studies and proposals for the New York Metropolitan District and the federal and state governments. Additionally, the organization is exploring options for ongoing green initiatives, mobility and transportation, workforce development and improved governance at the regional level. Other, far more powerful organizations are at work implementing improvements in area transportation and exploring solutions to the problems.

WHAT'S NEXT?

Where are we headed, in terms of urban organization and process? Predictions often prove off the mark, even when the scholarship is sound and the analysis persuasive. For instance, Kenneth Jacobs, author of the influential *Crabgrass Frontier*, found that his expectation of a decline in automobile use was sorely wrong. Despite the danger, some peering into the future is necessary. First, however, we must step back and look at the bigger picture. North Jersey is at the heart of the most important area of development in the country: megalopolis.

Megalopolis

For over half a century, something new and special has been developing along the country's northeast corridor. Jean Gottman labeled it megalopolis, and he describes this phenomenon as simply an urban area from Boston to Washington, D.C. But that doesn't cover it. The mixed urban-suburban-rural conglomeration extends beyond that to southern New Hampshire and Northern Virginia and from the Atlantic to the Appalachian foothills. It includes cities, suburbs and green spaces and even some farming enterprise. It is a special area that offers a unique way of life and land use, and its dominance in political, economic and cultural affairs gives it a special place in the nation and the world.

Since 1950, the U.S. census has divided the region into Standard Metropolitan Districts, which brings some order to the complexity but also some confusion. As previously mentioned, North Jersey is included as part of the New York SMD, but this presents many difficulties. The SMD does show us that there are five major cities (Baltimore, Boston, New York, Philadelphia and Washington) that compose megalopolis, each with more than one million people. In a sense, I-95 is a main street for America, running through all these cities, which became centers of industry by 1950 and have now become centers of finance and services. As local agriculture declined, farmland reverted into woodlands, which explains the amount of woodlands in North Jersey. But suburban sprawl constantly cuts into that, breaking down the green areas into strips and patches. This background is helpful in understanding the phenomenon of megalopolis, but a lot has changed in the last fifty years.

The power and impact of megalopolis was so great that many expected other parts of the nation to develop in a similar way. Garreau points to a selection of regions, notably the international concentrations centered on Seattle and Vancouver or Los Angeles–San Diego–Tijuana. He took the concept a step further and suggested that the growth of his selected regions would yield megalopolises that would become new functional "nations." Sociologists focused on the megalopolis phenomenon for a time until it became obvious that other, more structured ideas and proposals were more productive, as proved to be the case with the edge city concept.

Edgeless Cities

Garreau exerted considerable influence on urban studies for a time, but further study reveals that a lot of his basic facts were wrong. For instance, none of his New Jersey edge cities actually meets his criteria. Three of the ten he named had the five million square feet of office space, but the nearest significant mall was miles away. One review of Garreau's thirteen largest edge cities included interviews with several urban specialists. Some of the components of Garreau's model are clearly in evidence, but key arguments, such as "density is back" in the form of edge cities, do not work. According to Robert Lang, "Sprawl...never went away." The evidence simply did not prove Garreau's edge city theory.

Lang's study utilizes city-planning theory. He tries to find a path between the centrists and the de-centrists, where the centrists call for many centers in villages in the traditional city pattern while the decentrists emphasize the role of personal mobility and focus on residential areas without reference to traditional city arrangements. While cities are less central today, several downtown areas are enjoying a comeback, including Newark. Many people are seeking ways to become less dependent on the automobile, and companies find it useful to get back downtown because the talent pool is larger and more diverse (a result of increased educational opportunities). There is not a good label for this change, but there are a number of possible names, three of which we will discuss briefly.

Sprawl

Many scholars and observers point to a number of changes in urban areas to explain urban sprawl: the popularity and success of "big box stores" (such as Walmart), drive throughs (restaurants, banks and pharmacies), green fields (suburbs on raw land), gridlocks, ground covers (cheap buildings holding land for later development), manufactured homes, noise walls (found along freeways), theme cities (Las Vegas) and tract mansions. What are called growth corridors have been identified in North Jersey, particularly around Route 1, the Garden State Parkway, Route 80 and the Meadowlands. These are characterized by high-tech facilities and jobs and feature many pockets of commercial facilities. Thomas Stanbeck uses the label of metropolitan economics to describe regions that are characterized by increased growth of service-providing companies, local government facilities (such as convention centers) and growth in financial, insurance and real estate businesses. His data also highlights the role of secondary income for people in the form of interest, dividends, rents and transfer payments. Not everyone has to work for a living in today's economy, and those fortunate folks tend to relocate to new, developing areas rather than the traditional city.

Sprawl appears to be an inevitable consequence of population growth in North Jersey, as elsewhere. The question is whether it can, in some measure, be managed.

Virtual Cities

Several years ago, MIT architect–media professor William J. Mitchell raised the issue of how the shift from atoms to bits in the digital age would shape our cities and its buildings. There would be similarities; both the physical and the virtual city would have access (streets and portals), boundaries (fences and networks) and public and private spaces. But there would be differences as well; virtual campuses would replace schools, electronic malls would replace stores and telemedicine would serve in place of medical-care facilities. Public cyberspace would reduce face-to-face interaction, and distance would no longer bar people from social participation. The fate of the city of the future will depend on the successful creation and management of information rather than the effectiveness of transportation and communication capabilities. Mitchell expanded his thinking a decade later in another book, *Me++*, which describes how technological extensions transform people into cyborgs as a result of humanity's constant and instantaneous telecommunications and visual environments. He was a bit ahead of his time, but his foresight of how our technologies might impact our lives and living spaces is a wake-up call. The thought that our physical lives can change and explorations of what this might mean for the human experience is clearly a useful exercise.

Two very different scenarios are at work here: the rise of the megalopolis concentrating people in fewer places and the diminution of physical presence in favor of virtual reality and human cyber interaction. The two are seemingly irreconcilable images of the future.

The network society is an early product of the telecommunications revolution. According to Manuel Castells, networks are open sets of interconnected nodes, and this arrangement involves connectors, clustering and power laws that render the notion of finance capitalism less accurate than information capitalism because of the constant interactivity and space of information flows that challenge traditions of linearity, randomness and reductionism. The network theoretically allows virtual communities to gather around common interests, work or fantasies. But Castells agrees with those who argue that the advantages of personal acquaintance, shared understanding and relationships still allow people to interact face to face, what Castells calls place-based sociality. This suggests that middle-range, mesoregional dynamics could play important roles in solving current problems.

The rapid emergence of social media, considered by many to be a game changer, necessitates a note of caution. Visual and audio interactivity and participation offered by Facebook, Twitter and YouTube not only allow users to share but also allow them to share on multiple levels, rendering web pages static in comparison. Many believe that this sets the stage for entirely new levels of collaboration, creativity and knowledge creation. The balance could shift from place to a network, and that would have profound consequences for urban life.

Urban Revolution

Cities continue to draw many people, particularly the young and the optimistic who believe they offer great opportunity. In my lifetime, the urban riots of the 1960s (in Detroit, Newark and Watts) made the concept of the city none too appealing. Additionally, the financial crisis of the 1970s in New York suggested that cities offered great instability. I spent six weeks in New York going through securities training in 1984. During the drive from John F. Kennedy Airport to Manhattan, we passed several burned-out and abandoned cars. We also saw several vandalized and abandoned buildings on our way to our midtown hotel. And on the way to dinner that evening, we had to step around an intoxicated (drunk or drugged, I cannot say) man lying on the sidewalk. I left the city unimpressed.

New York at the time, in the words of Edward Glaeser, "appeared to be dying." Indeed, Glaeser notes that eight of the top ten cities in the United States had decreased in population at that point. A creature of industrialism, the city appeared to be obsolete in the age of information.

But people are still relocating to New York and other urban centers. Detroit is experimenting with urban farming, and the Newark-centered cities of North Jersey are reviving through gentrification and revitalization of their downtown areas. Additionally, the majority of Americans already live in urban areas, and suburbs and rural areas struggle to maintain some sense of promise for the future. The green movement is hastening the process. The city, with its massive transportation and high-rise apartments, requires less energy than either suburbs or rural areas where people are reliant on automobiles. Even more than that, the new urban revolution is "changing the world," according to Jeb Brugmann. New city systems are enjoying greater productivity, efficiency and economies of scale, and emerging models of planned cities and "smart" systems are being designed to meet the enduring needs of people rather than the needs of factories.

Metroburb

One model that offers reasonable solutions to current urban problems is the metroburb, a medium-sized area that encompasses older downtown areas, suburbs, green spaces and outlying territory. Paul Knox uses the term to describe vast, sprawling multinodal mixtures of central city, suburbs, employment and residential centers that meet the needs of the new "postsocial" lifestyle. Proximity is not always a necessity in the digital age, but face-to-face interaction and social trust remain keys to innovation and adaptation. The metroburb further enables clustered economic developments like Silicon Valley, Hollywood or New York's financial districts and allows the creation of new industries or the transformation of old ones as a result of people communicating and participating in regional learning.

An Immodest Proposal:
Newark Bay/Liberty City

Although there is not a major city in North Jersey, much less New Jersey, this could change. Newark, with its population of 277,000 people, along with Jersey City (248,000), Elizabeth (125,000), Bayonne (63,000) and Kearney (41,000), could collaborate on difficult inter-city issues as a step toward coming together into a single entity. They are contiguous, and all share access to Newark Bay. The new city population would start at 750,000, putting it ahead of Detroit, Milwaukee and other recognized cities. It would most likely have to happen through the democratic process, but the "home rule" tradition could serve to create something greater and, for once, not simply break up a larger town. The new city envisioned here would be much less complicated than New York and the several islands that compose it, even though major portions of three counties (Hudson, Essex and Union) would be impacted.

Ports, airports and other major transportation hubs are considered necessary for a city to thrive. This Newark Bay City would enjoy all three. Kasarda and Lindsay predict that an airport-centered city, or Aerotropolis, will characterize a new era, bringing about the decline of the automobile. Newark Liberty is arguably more accessible for New Yorkers than either of the city's two major

Luxury condos, Society Hill. *Photo by author.*

A working dock at Port Elizabeth. *Photo by author.*

airports. And the new city could surely land one or more television networks, stimulate various consolidations of public and private institutions and attract more businesses and sports franchises, some of which may even choose to call themselves something other than New York.

Obviously, considerable discussion and political activity would be required to get this item on the public agenda, as well as serious study of the political and economic advantages of large-city status to gauge the value of the endeavor. But the advantages of being a major city could overcome the disadvantages all around, save some office holders. The close proximity of some cities in New Jersey has assured their minor-city status, and only a few have ever received widespread recognition. The larger point is that while the city has not died, neither has it reached its full potential in North Jersey. Meanwhile, neither the state nor present political arrangements meet the region's needs. It's time to contemplate other options. Why not Newark Bay City?

CHAPTER 5

WHERE TO?
NORTH JERSEY AS PORTAL

Our highways look infected and our cities are empty sockets and our
Politics an oil slick six decades wide.
—*David Roth,* Living on the Edge

Many writers, current and past, depict North Jersey as something transitional—a passage or highway to something or somewhere else. Others dwell on the idea of place: dying urban centers, crowded tenements, toxic dumps, sprawling suburbs, dynamic communities and neighborhoods; or, by contrast, a locale where one can find stunning natural beauty in the hills, wetlands, lakes and forests. The contrasts are fascinating. The goal of this chapter is to show that seeing North Jersey as passage or simply a place is sufficient. It is the experience that matters.

GATEWAY OR THOROUGHFARE?

The image of a road, thoroughfare or turnpike is a recurring theme used to explain New Jersey, reflecting the importance of location and transportation for the state and, for that matter, for the county. The widespread usage of railroads in the state before the 1960s and the dominance of automobiles characterize the state for many observers.

As aforementioned, the region's location made it a strategic battleground and crossroads for the American Revolution. George Washington crossed the Delaware River and captured the Hessian troops at Trenton, and the Battle of Princeton took place in Greater North Jersey. But there were several additional battles and strategic marches in the area because of its position between New York and Philadelphia. And North Jersey's strategic value did not change with independence. The need for improved transportation became apparent during the War of 1812, when Britain instituted a naval blockade that disrupted trade in and through North Jersey. Internal transportation immediately became critical for commerce. Several new bridges across smaller rivers helped, but major river crossings at Jersey City, Camden and Trenton often had two to three hundred wagons awaiting ferries. Fortunately, the war was brief and the disruptions manageable. One response was the chartering of fifty-one turnpikes, an exceptional number for a small state and few of which proved profitable or sustainable. The next step, inspired by the progress of the Erie Canal, was the construction of canals.

In the 1820s, an engineering marvel was built to connect the Delaware River to North Jersey's ports and the ocean. The Morris Canal, envisioned by Morristown native George P. McCulloch and funded primarily by area investors, is 102 miles long and cuts through the mountains of the Highlands area. It opened in 1831 and provided transport for coal from Pennsylvania mines and beyond to the iron furnaces in northeast Jersey. Other goods traveled the route as well. Hamlets along the way, such as Boonton, Hackettstown, Little Falls and Montville, benefitted from the economic activity, developing new crops and products that could now reach markets and enjoying significant growth between 1840 and 1870.

A key portion of the canal ran through the Musconetcong Valley to what's now known as Lake Hopatcong. The valley was a sparsely settled region of the Highlands, and its soil was poorly suited to agriculture. Settlers quickly turned to other means of production, notably charcoal ironworks. Several forges and bloomeries (furnaces) turned out wrought iron. But the charcoal industry depleted woodlands, which, incidentally, encouraged farming as there was now clear land to farm on. The iron industry was in decline by the time the Morris Canal was built, but new fuel in the form of Pennsylvania coal breathed new life and caused some facilities to reopen. Other industries included apple orchards and fermented applejack, a popular product of the day, along with a few gristmills, sawmills and tanneries. Before the canal, transporting these products to the east was extremely difficult, and

The Morris Canal ends in Jersey City. *Postcard of painting*

oftentimes, more goods were sent southward to be sold in Philadelphia than to the northeast. The canal changed all that, reviving production in the valley and across Morris County.

The history of the canals overlaps with the early days of the railroad. John Cunningham, a prolific and influential publicist for the State of New Jersey, first got involved with local history by writing about the railroad industry in New Jersey. When he returned to the topic decades later, he elaborated on the economic impact the railroads had, and his work influenced many other writings on the significance of the railroad industry in North Jersey.

In returning to the question of New York's influence on North Jersey, the question of who created these pathways arises. Who were the industry's founders and investors? It appears that most of the initiators of early transportation improvements were Jerseyans. In the first decade of the country's history, bridges were built to increase accessibility. A few years later, toll-road turnpikes were established, and most of these were locally financed. The Morris Canal was also designed and organized by locals, but in addition to George McCulloch and another local man, three New Yorkers were listed as commissioners to receive subscriptions. Presumably, some New York monies went into the original investment, but when construction costs ran nearly twice the estimate, a completion loan was arranged. Interestingly, it came from Holland and was known as the Dutch loan. Still, continuing economic difficulties led to foreclosure in 1844. New owners bought the canal for $1 million, but stockholders and creditors lost money, as did the State of Indiana, which held the second mortgage on the canal. The new owners widened and improved the canal, and a more prosperous enterprise ensued, though the canal never produced much in the way of profits. In 1871, the canal was leased to the Lehigh Valley Railroad Company, a Pennsylvania firm wanting access to "tide waters."

Similar arrangements were typical for the first railroads. Private investors funded early railroad construction under state supervision. (This contrasts with Pennsylvania, where the state underwrote railroad construction.) The first operating line was the Camden & Amboy, which opened in January 1833 and used horse teams. The first steam engine, imported from England, went into service in September. Other railroad lines and companies followed, linking Paterson to Jersey City and Newark with New Brunswick. All of these lines were owned primarily by locals. Investment monies were hard to come by, and the information on the proposed projects was sparse and often less than trustworthy, even when local people led the effort. Investing across state lines came later.

One exception was the New Jersey Railroad & Transportation Company, which brought in New York financing for the Jersey City–New Brunswick line. But these early railroads operated under state charters that guaranteed them monopolies over their routes in return for fees paid to the state. According to John Cunningham, the legacy of this practice has two sides. For years, New Jersey had little need for additional taxation, but the price was a tradition of corruption and bribery over state-backed business ties that became a hallmark of New Jersey politics.

Peak railroad construction occurred between 1870 and 1900. Most of the eleven rail lines ran toward the urban port areas around Newark, and there were ferry links across the Hudson River to New York. Cheap ore from Pennsylvania disrupted North Jersey's iron production, but the area quickly adapted to metalworking, and many innovators developed new major products, such as Samuel Colt, the inventor of the Colt revolver. Transportation of people and freight now became widely available and relatively efficient and inexpensive. But the bustling industries of Jersey City, Newark and Paterson made up the primary market. The region clearly was a center of activity and not simply a transit point to New York. With more than two thousand miles of track in a small area, North Jersey rail traffic was by far the busiest and most dense in the nation.

Pennsylvania Railroad Station, Newark, circa 1907. *Postcard.*

The ferry *Leonia* was used to complete railroad trips across the Hudson River to New York. *Postcard.*

The Penn Railroad cut through the Palisades to reach the Hudson River. *Postcard.*

Getting across the barriers of the Hudson River and the cliffs of Bergen County proved a substantial but conquerable obstacle. The first opening through the ridge, known as the Bergen Cut, took five years to dig, and its first train passed through in 1838. The task ultimately was accomplished by building tunnels under the Hudson River, which was a major operation that involved the skills and knowledge of mining, tunneling and railroad building. The major figure in the work was DeWitt Clinton Haskin, an innovative New York engineer who utilized compressed air to help secure the tunnel from collapse. After careful study and with $10 million in subscriptions, he began work in 1874. Despite all precautions, a leak caused a collapse in 1880 and killed nineteen men. Stockholders forced a reorganization in 1888, bringing in a more experienced British firm, but another failure in 1892 caused a ten-year delay in the work. The tunnel was completed in 1903. Other railroad tunnels followed, but expectations for the railroad were not fully realized because of the public switch to the automobile for transportation.

Most of the state's early transportation activity was in North Jersey, where a rail network was in place by the 1840s, including lines to Somerville and Morristown. South Jersey established lines in the following decade and profited from the need for more links with Philadelphia. The burgeoning business then began attracting outside investment, particularly from Wall Street, already a vital financial center.

The impact of the railroad was rapid and dramatic. Manufacturing plants were established in the towns and villages along the rail lines. Farmers responded to the new and growing markets in additional towns and benefitted from easy and rapid transportation. Villages that had sprung up along the lines gradually grew into towns. Shops expanded into factories in Elizabeth, Newark and Paterson. Hoboken's seedy waterfront became a vibrant transportation hub with a steady stream of ferries taking people and goods to and from New York.

The Civil War created an economic boom for the railroad industry. The Rogers Locomotive complex in Paterson produced nineteen locomotives in three months, which was three times its normal pace. North Jersey became the center of America's Industrial Revolution. Following the war, new waves of immigrants arrived and were armed with a strong will to seize every opportunity to have better lives. Most of all, the railroad centralized production in the city. The populations of Elizabeth, Newark and Paterson all grew to 100,000. There were boom times and bad times, but the industrial experience defined this center of economic development into the twentieth century and through its first four decades.

This part of the story is well known, so much so that it is repeated in every book on the state's history. Less familiar is the larger impact of the railroad on the North Jersey territory. The rail lines forged a distinctive environment, described by John Stilgoe as the "metropolitan corridor," a phenomenon

Penn Depot, Jersey City. *Postcard.*

The Rubber and Bronze Works, Elizabeth, circa 1905. Most factories were located in the city and on the railroad. *Postcard.*

experienced along every main rail line. And North Jersey had the most dense concentration of railroads in the nation.

Between 1880 and 1930, the railroad transformed great chunks of the American landscape, creating no less than a fourth environment that was distinct from rural, urban and suburban realities. It was a new arrangement of space and structure, and it also involved a new lifestyle. This metropolitan corridor is much less visible today; in fact, it has to be sought out. But remnants can be found by looking for flat corridors with large run-down buildings, warehouses and grain elevators. Many depots are also still standing. These depots were once very important buildings for towns, but many are now empty or have been converted into restaurants or shops. Signs of remarkable engineering accomplishments can be found around water crossings and old depots, such as bridges, railyards and rail switches. In its heyday, Pennsylvania Railroad dug tunnels beneath the Hudson River and extended them to railyards on Long Island. Electrical lines and then diesels reduced the awful smoke and grime of earlier steam engines. The complex included industrial zones and agricultural zones, as well as Pullman cars, which provided luxurious travel for passengers. Depots also provided connections to

Pennsylvania Ferry and Depot, Jersey City, circa 1905. *Postcard.*

trolley lines, which in turn facilitated the growth of suburban areas where the prosperous could escape the city and enjoy large homes and gardens on tree-lined streets.

Towns and villages along the railroad routes prospered, and the overall impact of the railroad helped to shape American identity. Literature, the early cinema and popular culture had few themes of comparable influence. The longing of Johnny Cash's prisoner who was stirred by the train whistle was very different from Henry David Thoreau's feelings. Both, however, found the sound worthy of comment. Lionel toy trains were a rite of passage for American boys. They were manufactured primarily in North Jersey as well, leading the company to become the largest toy company in the world in the 1950s. And nowhere was the impact greater than in North Jersey, with its two-thousand-mile corridor.

There were alternative scenarios, of course. Railroads could create suburbs as well as cities, as the Bergen County experience demonstrates. County population grew steadily but slowly over the course of the nineteenth century, reaching only 78,441 in 1900. The growth spurt (73 percent) came in the first decade of the twentieth century (adding 38,000 people), and there was another increase in the 1920s. By 1930, the population had reached 365,000. But the railroad played a different role in Bergen County. Rather than feeding the city's industrial hunger, five new lines ran north into the rural area to create suburbs for people who desired the "country life." The result was a vast getaway for New Yorkers. There were still no cities

Broad Street in downtown Newark, early twentieth century. *Postcard.*

in Bergen County, and there were only a few scattered industries. But the impact on the area—and society—was nevertheless dramatic.

These suburban developments converged to create the sprawling urban region of North Jersey. People, factories and transportation hubs stimulated the growth of crowded cities, and Jersey City, Newark and Paterson grew dramatically during this time as we have seen. A 1930s study of New Jersey listed twenty towns of importance; most—with the exception of towns of special interest like Princeton or Atlantic City—were larger towns. Seven cities were at or above 100,000 in population. Only Camden (across the Delaware River from Philadelphia) in the south and Trenton in the central region were outside North Jersey. The largest cities by the numbers were Bayonne, Elizabeth, Jersey City, Newark and Paterson. Machine politics, a volatile economy, wealth creation and a polyglot culture all reflected the dynamism of the region and the era.

Cities dominate their region, but since North Jersey lacks a major city, was the region dominated by New York? Or did this close combination of five urban centers dominate North Jersey? Lewis Mumford credits New York with the capability of transforming "tribes and nations" into spheres of cooperation. A common culture absorbs the existing local culture. An infrastructure of power grids, communication and cultural institutions such as libraries and art centers overpower the periphery. But

The Firemen's Insurance Building reflected Newark ambitions. *Postcard.*

the story is not that simple. Newark competed for preeminence at times. The status and legacy of the Newark Public Library is testimony to the city's urge to become a dominant city. It can be argued that separation was more characteristic than unity. New York newspapers might be widely read by North Jerseyans, but local papers out circulate the elitist *New York Times*. In recent decades, the dominance of New York–based network television stations is a point for the New York story. The issue is not yet resolved. Meanwhile, the preeminence of the cities and railroads and the whole urban arrangement soon felt the impact of a new revolution in transportation: the automobile.

AUTOMOBILITIY

The automobile as we know it took some time to materialize. In the last years of the nineteenth century, a number of comparable vehicles powered by steam, electricity and gasoline engines competed against one another for success and leadership in the new industry. In 1895, there were only about 300 such vehicles in the country, but this grew to 78,000 by 1905. Pope Manufacturing in Ohio made 500 electric cars between 1895 and 1897, and Stanley began making steam-powered vehicles in Massachusetts. The breakthrough in mass production came between 1908 and 1927, when more than 15 million Model T Fords rolled off the assembly line in Detroit. Early models sold for $950, but the price fell with the rise of productivity, dropping to $360 in 1916. In 1929, 5.5 million cars were produced and a total of 26.5 million were registered in the United States. The country would never be the same.

In many ways, manufacturing the automobile was the easy part; it was making them available to customers that was tricky. The earliest manufacturers made a few cars and sold them directly, sometimes by mail with shipment to the buyer in a crate. The best prospects for dealers were found among bicycle-shop owners, where cars usually were a sideline to the main business. Cars were bought and sold for cash since they were somewhat problematic, and many were often abandoned along the side of the road. By the 1920s, a modern system of direct dealerships emerged across the country, and these usually featured showrooms and parts and service departments.

The road to supremacy had its bumps. Several car manufacturers folded during the Depression, and countless numbers of car dealerships followed suit, dropping from a high of fifty-one thousand in 1929. Things were even worse during World War II, when no cars were produced for stateside use, but those who managed to survive got their reward in the postwar boom.

The automobile industry took off after the Second World War, largely because of the millions of veterans returning to the States who required a vehicle to commute to work, school or their suburban homes. Smaller brands, however, struggled slightly in trying to compete against the Big Three automakers. Kaiser-Fraser, Studebaker, Nash, Hudson, Packard and others made a run, but all of these companies would fail or merge by 1970.

To handle the surge of business, dealers built larger facilities, added professional sales and service people and followed their customers as they used their new "ride" to move out of the city into suburbs and outlying areas. By 1977, five hundred dealers in North Jersey were selling, on average, over three hundred new cars a year and enjoying the benefits of a $5 million business, a great deal of money for the time.

Essentially, the automobile killed the dominance of the railroad. It allowed the population to move away from the city and bypass the downtown factories, and it also stimulated an entirely new economic infrastructure and landscape. Once again, New Jersey led the way. By the 1960s, the new highway system created a high amount of traffic that exceeded the traffic of any other state highway system. In fact, New Jersey's traffic density is several times that of Pennsylvania and New York.

John Cunningham's image of a main road for America became a reality with the construction of the New Jersey Turnpike. This highway, the busiest in the nation, gave the state a new identity. The turnpike quickly became a new symbol for New Jersey. Rutgers University professors Angus Gillespie and Michael Rockland chronicle the importance of the turnpike and explain much of the impact of the automobile in *Looking for America on the New Jersey Turnpike*. Gillespie and Rockland argue that the turnpike was the road that created many of New Jersey's stereotypes. Many people are surprised to learn that the road was not built in the 1950s along with President Eisenhower's Interstate Highway System. The New Jersey Turnpike was authorized in 1948 by Governor Alfred Driskoll and was built using bond funding based on tolls so the many tourists and visitors into New Jersey could help pay the tab. It was essentially built in less than two years, and the 148-mile road was opened in January 1952. In many ways, the interstate system followed the Jersey example.

North Jersey is economically, geographically and ethnically diverse, and the opening of the turnpike made it even more so. It disrupted communities and, for many, removed any sense of belonging, leaving little to hold the state together as an entity. Gillespie and Rockland suggest the turnpike is "the machine in the garden." Exit numbers became significant directions for travelers and all who would attract their attention. Although designed and built for efficiency, the road highlighted some of the worst elements of Jersey life, from factory smokestacks, refineries and landfills to miles of uniform mass-produced postwar housing. Such was the memory for many, including this writer, who drove the route to New York from North Carolina in 1964. Herein lies the question of whether Jersey is just a passage or portal to somewhere else.

ASPHALT NATION

We are still learning to what the extent the automobile changed our way of life. The American landscape was transformed in the post–World War II years. Downtown business centers and residential districts lost their middle-class clienteles, and these areas became either working-class or immigrant neighborhoods or went into severe decline. Many early suburbs shared that fate; residential values plummeted as minority populations in these areas increased. Strip malls and advertising billboards turned pleasant drives into cluttered distractions. Drive-ins, including banks, movies, quick stops and gas stations, became ubiquitous features of most thoroughfares. Gridlock triggered the construction of new roads, spreading the joy of the new suburban lifestyle farther and farther from urban centers When the mass-produced automobile rolled off the assembly lines in the 1920s, it was assumed that the city and the Model T Ford would complement each other and usher in a wonderful new life. Indeed, the gas-powered automobile would become the heart of twentieth-century life. In the 1950s, President Eisenhower initiated an Interstate Highway System that linked the North to the South and the East Coast to the Pacific Ocean. In the beginning, these concrete ribbons only cost $1 million per mile, but by the end, the cost was up to $2 billion.

The arrival of foreign cars, most of which came from Japan and Germany, caused some automakers anxiety. By the late 1980s, many automobile

A traffic jam in downtown Union Township, 1960s. *William F. Augustine Photo Collection, Special Collections, Alexander Library, Rutgers University.*

companies feared that the Japanese would buy up the country just as they had Radio City Music Hall. By this time, the cons of the automobile had become more than evident. Because so many people were tied to the highway network, the institution of family suffered. In North Jersey, the older urban centers continued to decline, and the area became a beehive of roads, highways and superhighways. The Garden State Parkway is one example. On the bright side, this road opened the New Jersey shore to visitors and helped Atlantic City become a tourist Mecca with its gambling casinos and resort hotels. The automobile also secured the success of shopping malls.

Perhaps the best evidence of the power of the automobile is the determination by some of the best minds in the country to overcome obstacles to the vehicle's limitations. Engineers and awesome infrastructure projects solved problem after problem and allowed the automobile to help transform North Jersey—and American—society. A series of events followed, all of which have made North Jersey what it is today.

1927   The Holland Tunnel opens.

1931   The George Washington Bridge opens.

1937   The Lincoln Tunnel opens its first tube.

1945   The Lincoln Tunnel opens its second tube.

1952   The main sections of the New Jersey Turnpike open.

1957   The third tube of the Lincoln Tunnel opens.

1962   The lower level of the George Washington Bridge is completed.

This steady drumbeat of infrastructure improvements supported vehicular travel and stimulated North Jersey's growth over the years. The population of the eight North Jersey counties rose sporadically but continued to grow every decade. With the exception of Hudson County, which suffered a decline in population, the region as a whole grew by nearly half (46.5 percent) in thirty years, from 2.77 million in 1930 to 4.06 million in 1960. Another issue must be addressed: how was the cooperation required for this infrastructure creation realized?

PORT AUTHORITY

Occasional and sometimes bitter quarrels between New York and New Jersey occurred during the nineteenth century. There were even exchanges of gunfire between agents of the two sides, and New Yorkers burned New Jersey piers more than once to stop Jerseyans from trespassing on "their" Hudson River. This hurt the commerce of the region. By 1920, the Port of New York was stagnating, and North Jersey shared its pain. The lack of links (not counting the two railroad tunnels beneath the Hudson River) between the two states was generally seen to be the problem. Bi-state and tri-state commissions plotted and planned various solutions. A highway tunnel under the Hudson River was considered, but before any action could be taken, local politics had to be neutralized. There was little support for that, as the newspapers served local interests above all. There were few championing for a regional perspective.

Nevertheless, in 1921, the state legislatures agreed to the establishment of the New York Port Authority, to be governed by a board of directors whose members were evenly divided between New York and New Jersey and appointed to rotating terms by the two state governors. Its prospects appeared dim at first; other commissions were already at work. The idea was presented to business and political communities as bringing expertise and guidance to help solve problems that would otherwise remain problems. It was innovative, and the idea was based on London's Port Authority. Despite many challenges and difficulties from city councils and corporate boardrooms, as well as the White House, the authority ultimately worked, changing the way the entire region operated.

Businessmen and politicians made the port authority possible, but the essential ingredient was the sustained and stable leadership of a few individuals, notably Julius Henry Cohen, Othmar Ammann and Austin Tobin, who weathered the storms, made the authority successful and oversaw its operation. Cohen was an architect; Ammann, an engineer; and Tobin, an attorney. But all proved to be visionary public (and quasi-governmental) entrepreneurs, and together, they left impressive monuments to human skill and accomplishment, including the Lincoln Tunnel, George Washington Bridge, the Port Authority Bus Terminal and the World Trade Center's twin towers, as well as three major airports and numerous other bridges, tunnels and structures.

The endeavor was never about New York alone, as reflected by the New York Port Authority being renamed the Port Authority of New York and New Jersey in 1976 to indicate the equal participation of each state. New York needed New Jersey—more specifically North Jersey—and New Jersey benefitted by collaborating with New York to an extent none of the founders of the authority could have imagined. Indeed, more of the drive and money came from the New York side of the river, but New Jersey chose to participate despite anxieties of being "used" by its larger neighbor. But before the authority's work was done, projects in New Jersey, such as developing Newark Airport and Port Newark, aroused envy among Manhattan businessmen who felt that the organization was favoring New Jersey at their expense.

The increased traffic and commerce provided by the new port authority created dynamic growth and great wealth in North Jersey. Political and

Newark Airport, which opened in 1928, was the first major airport in the metropolitan region and quickly became one of the busiest in the country. Pictured here is an early Holiday Airlines carrier. *Postcard.*

business groups participated, and this was sometimes helpful but often not. Neither the business nor the public side can claim the credit. But one lesson is clear: for all its wonders, unfettered democracy can be debilitating when it comes to solving complex problems. A second lesson follows: on their own, business interests focus too much on competition and too little on collaboration. Government intervention at a level other than state and local interests is one key to success, a reality that is too quickly forgotten by both politicians and corporate interests. North Jersey participated in a partnership that served as a model for the rest of the country.

REGIONAL ENDEAVORS

Academics and professional planners promote regional solutions to complex problems. The logic of knowledgeable planners continues to hold broad appeal. But regional successes, even at a modest level, remain the exception, not the rule. A large-scale study of regional politics and initiatives in the

New York metropolitan region suggests that in order to succeed, regional endeavors must address a special problem and purpose, be agreed to by all the states involved and be approved at the federal level. Even then, it is critical to find or create a new source of revenue and to deal with an issue of little interest to local governments.

There are many regional authorities in New Jersey. There were 223 by the end of the twentieth century that dealt with special problems or opportunities between state and local levels or across political boundaries. Solid waste management is a typical and continuing problem, mostly because of the number of complexities involved and the difficulties they present to municipalities; yet state efforts to establish county control over this issue met with marginal success. School consolidation never gained much traction in the state, in contrast with New York, where extensive consolidation was accomplished. One more example of the power of the underlying assumptions and philosophy of home rule is available in the efforts to revive the west Hudson shore in the 1970s and 1980s. Careful plans were developed, including three state initiatives. The goal was to assure walkways along the riverfront, with housing and the inclusion or addition of schools and public services. But local politicians, responding to pressures from developers and financial interests, did not implement the plans. Instead, luxury offices and condominiums were built, and there was little public space or affordable housing. The City of Hoboken was the exception. It controlled the developers and kept skyscrapers from ruining people's view of the New York skyline. The communities that failed to block the high-rise buildings soon saw their construction, but those communities that were determined to stop them succeeded. The struggle between the business drive and quality of life issues is deep and abiding, and the economic-political nexus rarely produces outstanding achievements.

PORTAL?

A portal is an entry point, an imposing gateway into something else such as a public building or a computer system. In the information age, "home" web pages often serve as an entry point—a portal for gathering information that is supplemented with links and search engines to additional worlds of data, opinion and sales information.

The creation of the turnpike and construction of airports add to the sense of movement established by North Jersey's railroads, bridges and tunnels. Gillespie and Rockland insist that the dreary turnpike superhighway signals people to "move on," and Rockland adds that the George Washington Bridge symbolizes a gateway or portal. It is New York's primary connection to North Jersey and to the rest of the continental United States; North Jersey serves as a portal to New York and the world beyond. Its traffic is two-way instead of one. When the many facilities (bridges, tunnels and terminals) of the port authority are added, the totality becomes inescapable. It suggests that North Jersey is more of a function than a place. In a very real sense, North Jersey is a networked transportation hub that is in a constant state of transformation and passage and not just in regard to transportation. The image is powerful, meaningful and contains much truth. But North Jersey is more than that; we cannot rest here.

An interesting new vision that was recently proposed is of an airport-centered transportation system that also serves as a business and residential hub. "Aerotropolis" is the idea of John Kasarda and Greg Lindsay and has already been mentioned. Globalization is the underlying force at play in this scenario, as people need to collaborate more with colleagues in another state or country than with their neighbors. The second underlying force behind the idea is the decline of the suburb, which necessarily accompanies the decline of the automobile.

Traveling or visiting a new place can have a significant impact on a person. Experience is important, and we must go in with all our senses. "When the mind is in motion in this way, the experience of travel changes," said Tony Hiss. It enables people to "enter a different part of their own minds." Even short distances can bring one to very different places. In his book *In Motion*, Hiss uses the commute from New York to North Jersey on the New Jersey Transit Rail, which is an eight-minute trip from Penn Station, as an example. According to Hiss, the trip can be made from Manhattan on a lunch break. He calls the better use of existing and abandoned railway paths "parkwaying." Certainly traveling, or passing through portals, is a way of understanding the North Jersey experience. But does that capture the character of the region?

The testimony of creative writers and memoirists embellishes our theme. Specific model automobiles and travel by auto are prominent features in both Frederick Reiken's *Lost Legends of New Jersey* and Kristen Buckley's memoir *Tramps Like Us*. Travelogues are a popular folk-culture genre. Anecdotes of people leaving Jersey to "go West" or escape the East's heavy traffic and

Table C

Mobility Status of Resident Population: 2008

	Different Total	Same County	Different County	Same State	Differ't State	Abroad
U.S.	15.0 %	9.2 %	5.7 %	3.3 %	2.4%	.6 %
NJ	9.9 %	5.8 %	4.0 %	2.4 %	1.7 %	.7 %

taxes are commonplace. They can also be misleading. Recent census data on residential changes, however, show something quite different.

People in Jersey moved less in 2007 than people in any other state. New York came close, as 10.5 percent of its population had moved to a different house before 2008.

CONCLUSION

Sometimes, a transition occurs but quickly fades. An example is the story of Fort Lee's time as the center of the movie industry for two decades, starting in 1907. Fort Lee is on the Palisades and was then composed of rural areas and several small villages. Filmmaker William Fox led his crews (and other filmmakers in later years) across the Hudson River to Fort Lee, where he filmed many classic moves. Within a few years, he and others grew tired of the steep fees demanded by the Edison Trust for use of the kinetoscope and moved to sunny Hollywood.

While viewing New Jersey as a passage, a sojourn or a portal is interesting, it does not satisfactorily explain New Jersey's role as a place. Many issues remain open and unsettled. In the fall of 2011, discussions about North Jersey as a factor in transportation included its partnership with New York as a trade center, and there was also some consideration of an additional tunnel or bridge to accommodate growing rail traffic.

The New York–New Jersey Port is considered a single entity, and data is most often provided for the entire complex rather than its constituent parts. The port is a lively center of commerce; exports totaled $136.3 billion and imports $218.1 billion in 2010 alone. These figures amount to more than

A Palisade bluff overlooking the Hudson River. *William F. Augustine Photo Collection, Special Collections, Alexander Library, Rutgers University.*

10 percent of the total imports and exports for the nation and render the port first in U.S. exports and second in imports behind Los Angeles. The concentration around Newark Bay is distinctive, and the cities' port-handling capabilities continue to expand. The commercial activity at Newark Liberty Airport adds to the economic output. Thus, we see that the Newark Bay region is a dynamic economic engine, and it could possibly lead to larger local government collaboration.

The second issue revolves around the project to improve rail traffic from North Jersey to Manhattan. A massive ARC (Access the Region's Core) project to facilitate fast-rail service in the future was cancelled by Governor Christie amid a wave of criticism. But rail transport is increasing, not only in the way of freight but in commuter traffic as well. A less expansive gateway project is still under consideration, but projected costs are still high. Interestingly, this writer found bus transportation faster, more comfortable and less expensive in commuting from Morris County to Queens by way of Manhattan. Bus travel is up, but the image is not made appealing in the literature and publicity of the New Jersey Transit Authority. Whatever the preferred mode, transportation remains a central component of the North Jersey–New York relationship.

CHAPTER 6

PLACE OR EXPERIENCE?

*You know why they call it the Garden State don't you? It's like
the Garden of Eden; everyone is from there originally but no one
you meet actually lives there anymore.*
—Irina Reyn

How does a space become a place? How does a run-down bar become
a neighborhood hangout? How does a dot on a map become a tourist
hot spot while a beautifully designed restaurant stands empty?

An interesting field of inquiry has emerged in the last few decades
as a result of increased study of the role of "place" in human thought,
culture and well-being. The topic is multidisciplinary and, consequently,
does not enjoy the acceptance of an established discipline of study. Some
of the ideas involved can be traced back to Aristotle, who wondered
about place but decided it was too complicated to explain and didn't.
Lewis Mumford also contributed to the discussion of place with his book
The City in History. He explains how cities develop a larger, common
culture that uses its mass communication to absorb local art, culture and
history. The work of historian Pierre Nora is also influential, as Nora
explains the role of memory in making a place something special to the
people who live there or care about it. The study of place then involves
history, geography, anthropology and psychology, as well as architecture,
city planning, landscape design, sustainability and aesthetics. Although
North Jersey is a region with boundaries (even if not widely accepted

as such), a relatively long history and a rich variety of experiences, the question of its status as a place remains at issue. The question is intriguing and the story illuminating.

How people use and experience space and place varies by culture. In *The Hidden Dimension*, Edward Hall explores the preferred distances between people, styles of communication and how space is visualized as topics of study regarding the influences people have on space and place and vice versa. "Space" is generally a neutral term, unless touching on exploration beyond earth. Place is much more complicated because it combines both personal and geographic connotations. A given place will have a locatable longitude and latitude, a topography and either natural or human-made appearance and features. It may or may not have a story, often an oral history or folklore, but now these histories are usually written. Place also plays a defining role in providing economic opportunity. One's quality of life and career opportunities are determined by where one grows up. People are the product of economic segregation and sprawl created by the American policies regarding land use, urban development and homeownership. In order to change the process of how space is used, one must understand this social reality.

North Jersey's diversity makes it complicated to consider it as a distinctive single place. It is a region, so it is a place in a very basic sense, but it is difficult to categorize. North Jersey features various types of terrain, from mountains to a coastal plain. The diversity of its people is even more remarkable, and all around the region are pockets of concentrated ethnic groups—Italians, Portuguese, Cubans and Turks, to name a few. Creating common cause is complicated by this reality because there are so many groups with different interests and so many communities with different environmental concerns. On the other hand, the density and small size of the region is one reason there is no real city in North Jersey.

THEORIES, TOWNS AND CITIES

There are reasons why communities have sprung up in certain places and why some flourish and others have failed. One model, called the "central place theory," presents the idea that a general store, a village, a town or a city exists to provide goods and services to its area. The size of the "center" is determined by the variety and value of the goods made available. A single store or small strip mall might provide a few basics for a neighborhood, such as bread, milk, a newsstand or a deli. In a town, there are more goods and more services available to residents: after-hours healthcare facilities, postal services, schools, a city hall, barbershops and beauty shops, a greater selection of foodstuffs and even some access to transportation elsewhere, such as a bus station or a car dealer. People will travel farther for these items. A city provides a much greater range: varieties of clothing, furniture, appliances, job opportunities, auto dealerships, hospitals, professional services such as attorneys, cultural and entertainment centers and more comprehensive government activities and medical services.

The proximity of North Jersey's cities helps explain why none of them grew to become a major metropolitan city. As we have seen, Newark, Jersey City and Elizabeth are all adjacent to one another, which means they lack room to expand. Each one of these small city centers developed industries that attracted workers to their central areas and allowed these places to experience population growth. But the difference in size between these small cities and surrounding towns was not sufficient for any of the three to develop the high level of goods and services characteristic of a larger city. Despite the fact that they drew tourists and new residents, that attraction was diminished by adjacent towns of significant size. A few institutions overcame the odds; the outstanding Newark Public Library is a remarkable example, but such exceptions don't invalidate the rule. A good theory can be a very practical thing.

What makes some places actual places is an image, shared experiences and a good story. Nora's concern about the loss of place results from what he sees as the loss of memory caused by the "acceleration of history"; the disruption of long-lasting peasant and commercial cultures by the speed of change; and the effort to identify heroes in order to create a formal history. As it develops, an official or accepted history wipes out human and tribal memory, unless preserved by deliberate effort. Such effort often takes the form of local celebrations, anniversaries and histories grounded in archives. For North Jersey, there is a plethora of stories but no overarching narrative that ties it all together. Perhaps this study can serve as a starting point and stimulate such development.

There are 227 municipalities in North Jersey, and a good number of them have their own historians. Places with relatively little documented history have their accounts, which are oftentimes fragmented and describe homes, buildings and crossroads that survive only in the memory of elders, essays from historical societies or faded photographs. Montville, for example, does not have a downtown area and no real center. There are several small strip malls and a business park on a main thoroughfare (Highway 46) but nothing approaching an identity. Economic-development efforts focus on sections of highways, such as Highway 46 or 202, and city facilities are scattered across the township. The main post office is in an obscure location and is not easily accessible for most people. One village in the township, Towaco, is notable for having a train station and nearby post office. Pine Bluff is another village within the town.

Nearby Parsippany, which is a relatively large North Jersey municipality consisting of fifty thousand people and is officially known as Parsippany–Troy Hills, is even more dispersed than Montville. Within it are two more villages: Tabor (which began as a Methodist summer camp) and Lake Hiawatha (though it is actually identifiable as a town as it has a busy main street, a variety of stores, a small but busy library and a large grocery store). One can drive through these places, but unless you keep a sharp lookout for obscure signs or business names, you may not know which town or village you are passing through.

There is an intriguing twist to the story. In 2007, *Money Magazine* named Montville number thirteen in its rankings of "Best Places (Small Towns) to Live in the U.S.," and in 2009, the magazine ranked the town twenty-first in the nation. In 2011, *Money* listed Montville as the number one "best small town" in New Jersey, despite its dispersed nature and lack of notable places or symbols. But there is another dimension: the per capita income for the community was an estimated $58,021 in 2008 (well above the national average), and no one living in poverty was identified in the town. The population is 85.0 percent white, 12.5 percent Asian and has a smattering of other racial groups. Montville is all about conditions of plenty, safety and comfort, and some see this as the good life, but in truth, the township hardly qualifies as a "place" because it does not engage residents or inspire their serious emotional involvement in local affairs. This suggests that importance of place can come second to experience; it also illustrates the reality of "economic segregation" in America.

Paterson is a very different place. Located a few miles east of Montville, it is certainly a city (though, as previously noted, nowhere near the greatness of a metropolitan city). It has its historians and industries and has, in the past, experienced labor difficulties, namely the great Silk Strike of 1913.

It has also been called home by various writers and artists, most notably William Carlos Williams. The story of Newark is one of commerce, as well as racial tension. In fact, the city hosted one of the greatest civil uprisings in America during the twentieth century. Additionally, Newark has been described as "resilient" in its adaptability in coping with declining property values (and the corresponding decline in tax revenues) accompanied by sharp declines in population. Great events or great monuments are not required, however, for a town with history or character to leave its tracks in the minds of people who grow up there. Events can also stimulate study and reporting, as the 1955 flood of the Delaware River did. This is not a recent trend, by the way; over one hundred years ago, the local Women's Auxiliary published a history of Nutley in Essex County, which, at the time, was a new commuter haven only fourteen miles from New York. The town flourished and attracted several prominent people from the city after the railroad established a connection in 1872. It remains a thriving township today and has a population of thirty thousand.

Interestingly, Americans cling to an idealized image of the small town where everyone knows their neighbor and pretty much everything that goes on in the community. That image, according to Richard Lingeman, shows the lasting influence of the idealized New England town. In the Virginia plantation tradition, conversely, the town was much less important; society was decentralized around the economic (farming) function. The ideal of the small, homogenous community faded in North Jersey—that is, if it ever took hold—with the continuous arrival of new immigrants and the rise of materialist motivations.

During America's period of industrialism, two kinds of cities emerged. At one extreme was Jersey City, which has many row houses, tenements and smoky factories crisscrossed first by railways and later by highways. In the mid-twentieth century, it was said to have "no center and no character." There were two shopping areas, one park and one hospital area, but it had little life of its own and was clearly a place to pass through but not to stay. At the other end of the spectrum is what Mumford calls the great "world city," which brings "tribes and nations" into spheres of cooperation. Such cities create common cultures that absorb the local and the provincial with a higher level of art, power grids and regional communication (now television stations), as well as museums and libraries. The problem for North Jersey was the absence of such a city within its boundaries and the proximity of an actual world city on the other side of the river. This is a big factor when considering the issue of whether North Jersey is part of

New York. There, as I've touched on, is a shared, unique culture, and this evidence suggests that North Jersey is indeed part of that city. But there are other factors to consider.

After the City

What comes after the city? One answer is "nowhere." The automobile became the "machine in the garden," according to James Kuntsler, and it unraveled the suburb as surely as it disrupted the city. When there is rapid and scattered construction "everywhere," that place becomes "nowhere." We long for special places but participate in the sprawl and growth that obliterate them. One proposal is to re-create neighborhoods and communities in order to "check" the process and save what is left of the countryside. Cities are shaped by their transportation systems, and those dominated by the automobile become fractured and incoherent, spewing their sprawl all about. Today, we live anywhere, anytime, with anybody we choose; traditional community survives primarily in our memories.

Meyrowitz offers a different explanation of the loss of "place," suggesting mass media is to blame. Television created an entirely new social environment by changing "who knows what about whom." Barriers fall as children learn about adult behavior, men and women about each other's stratagems and the public about the fallibility of politicians, institutions and celebrities. As groups develop new identities, different social roles and behaviors emerge and become dominant; at the same time, place loses importance for an increasingly nomadic, self-reliant population, which, out of necessity, becomes more tolerant of differences. As place shrinks in importance, so does the distinctiveness of traditional groups.

The quest for place continues, and it is far from moribund. A key part of that quest is the search and exploration of community. Ray Oldenburg explores the lack of informal gathering places and promotes the understanding and development of "third places." These are neutral grounds, accessible leveling places that facilitate conversation and interaction. Many can be found in the form of commercial enterprises, such as bars, cafés and coffee shops. These places serve as hangouts, which people crave. These physical environments are a force, Oldenburg argues, in the tradition that humans fashion their environments and vice versa.

Place, Passage, Experience

In *A Good Place to Live,* Terry Pindell addresses the problem of finding community by visiting and spending time in towns and cities across the country recommended to him by friends and other contacts who understood what he sought to do. He provides chapters on "winning" places and begins with Santa Fe, what he uses as a standard for comparison. He then journeyed around the country to towns of various regions. The majority of his ideal spots were, interestingly, college and university towns, such as Ithaca, New York; Burlington, Vermont; Charlottesville, Virginia; and Missoula, Montana. Many of the places he visited featured shops that were locally owned and operated and large residential areas, and both of these are of major importance in considering the role of community in regard to place, as are pedestrian access, parking, public transport, renovated older buildings and some form of entertainment.

The role of people in a place and how it is experienced cannot be overemphasized. Memory is key to the value placed on a place or experience of a place, and therefore, emotion comes into play in the selection and retention of something as memorable. We are social creatures, and human impact stirs emotion far more frequently than does landscape or memorial (with the exception of a sacred symbol). The depth of the role that place can play in the human psyche is described as "topophilia," or love of the local landscape. Elements of this emotional pull can be aesthetic (a view), kinesthetic (the "feel" of the environment) or cognitive (awareness of the local history and story). Topophilia is not normally an overwhelming emotion, but it can be substantial. And while the emotion is generally developed in resistance to the influence of the city, many people eventually transfer their feelings to the city, seeing it as representing enormous human achievement and accordingly worthy of great respect and attachment.

Richard Florida provides a different perspective on place in his best-selling book *Who's Your City?* He asserts that our choice of where we live is of enormous importance in regard to education, profession and life partner. Furthermore, what he refers to as superstar cities (San Francisco, Seattle and Bergen-Passaic in North Jersey) are important in attracting and stimulating creativity and innovation and are second only to mega regions such as Boston, New York, Washington or Tokyo. He stresses that place is a "central axis of our time" and offers guidance for the creative class, his new social and intellectual elite, by pointing to such factors as openness, aesthetics, safety, economic opportunity and physical security as very important for their way of life.

EXPERIENCE AND PLACE

Florida implicitly addresses the role of experience in the importance of place for many people. Creative work, which adds value to many endeavors, is social and participatory; it's not about isolated work or observation. He points to the large number of people who commute forty-five minutes or more to work as an expression of the importance of place in work and personal life. Tony Hiss, on the other hand, is quite explicit: place is something we experience. In his book *The Experience of Place*, he stresses "attending to" and being aware of our environment as an important skill to develop. We should broaden our senses and engage in "simultaneous perception" rather than focusing and narrowing our senses to a stream of consciousness. Such attention pays dividends; we can understand a place, be it a park, bus terminal or department store, by observing what people do there. In the countryside, it is not just scenery that appeals to people but the working environment as well. The revival of "working landscape" (such as farming) in both city spaces and countryside attests to a new appreciation for what can be done in and with a place. New approaches such as regional planning have protected parts of New York and North Jersey along the west bank of the Hudson River by utilizing a planning model similar to those used during the Depression era. In essence, place is about doing and not just seeing.

Generally, a sense of place is related to something smaller than a great city. The city disrupts the attachment to the local with the power of its transportation system. The automobile is a great example of this. The great roads and raised highways built in the last half of the twentieth century shattered the sense of place in the central city but did not replace it with anything that people identify with. Some call this the death of place, as it leaves only fractured, incoherent spaces and thoroughfares. The connections between people are what characterize community, and that was lost in the exhaust fumes of the automobile. The North Jersey adherence to "home rule" was a defense mechanism to keep the "city" in check. People liked the idea of keeping some continuity and familiarity in their lives and avoiding absorption into larger, less comprehensible cities.

Invisible Landscape

Place is more than a landmark, a memorable view or a town with sidewalks. Place has its maps, both on paper and mobile LED screens. Some are even cognitive, branded in the minds of residents both current and past. The key to place is more than the picturesque building, monument or street; it is the fusion of the physical with the mind's memory or use of it. More than that, it is a story, often a folktale, history or essay. Professor Kent Ryden is particularly taken with the essayists who balance the perspective of insider and outsider, describe both the built and natural landscape and fuse geography and mind into a dynamic account of the visible and invisible landscape. It's not just the physical but the experience and meaning of the place that completes this vision.

Place can be created. Landscape designers seek to create places all the time in yards, gardens and parks. And the skill and sensitivity for understanding and cultivating such a place can be developed. The goal is to provide an experience to the dweller or visitor, but according to Ray Garcia, the emotional reaction and memory produced from this establishment of place is not necessarily a long-term feeling. Garcia himself works and lives in other towns but has a sense of Montville, where he tutors a young student. For him that personal experience trumps place in the competition for heart and mind. But both experience and place are the basis for another kind of landscape that allows for the development of sustainability.

Worth Sustaining

Place also has an important role in the existing economy. According to a view popularized in the 1970s, a balanced economy is a healthy economy and more sustainable. A small but influential book by E.F. Schumacher entitled *Small Is Beautiful* presents the argument that smaller, more appropriate technologies are healthier for humans and the earth and more sustainable. The guidelines for green buildings established by the U.S. Green Building Council illustrates this view, and the council gives points for new structures that use local materials or those produced within a two-hundred-mile radius to reduce energy required for transportation. Global warming is ratcheting this issue into greater prominence. Al Gore's sobering message in *An Inconvenient Truth* has had enormous impact on Americans and people from other countries. Many are now accepting the idea that the key to sustainability is the design and use of products that require less material and energy to produce and are designed to be regenerated into more advanced products instead of simply being recycled as scrap. Recycling is just a band-aid on the wound; the goal has to be design that allows used products to be recycled into higher-level goods. Organizations must contribute to the upkeep of ecology and not simply take from it.

Local economics and sustainability add important conversations to the topic of place. Local economic activity challenges the perception that extractive products add the greatest value. The expansion of local business and supply relationships, creation of jobs, use of local building products and foodstuff and reduction of energy use all have substantial value to the local business economy by keeping capital local rather than shipping it elsewhere. Sustainability is defined as meeting the needs of the present generation without compromising the ability of future generations to meet their own needs. On the surface, the concept appears to run directly counter to the goals of growth and development, but such is not necessarily the case. In 1987, a United Nations World Commission on Environment and Development report entitled "Our Common Future" proposed that sustainable development be considered as an achievable balance between social equity, economic growth and ecological concerns. This argument revives the issue of enterprise versus quality. Perhaps a balance can be found, and there has been some achievement along those lines, as demonstrated by the work and success of the Meadowlands Commission. Thinking locally is the key to progress on this issue.

It is worth noting that New Jerseyans see the state as a good place to live, though that perception is on the decline. A Monmouth University survey finds that the number of people who feel the state is an excellent or good place to live has slipped from a high of 84 percent in 1987 (when Tom Kean was governor) to 63 percent in 2007, and that figure has not changed in the last five years. Significantly, New Jerseyans' confidence in the state's government has declined comparably, from 74 percent in 1984 to 53 percent in 2010. While not greatly distressed about conditions in the state, few feel confident that their state government will be able to solve the problems we face. On the upside, the region has a surprising quantity and quality of natural ecology, including wetlands, forest tracts and diverse wildlife. The state has successfully protected more than 100,000 acres in North Jersey.

For many New Jersey communities, the hill to sustainability is a steep climb. Many towns must deal with brownfields, which are abandoned or underutilized industrial sites that are largely polluted. Occasionally, these sites are valuable enough to warrant the expense of cleanup, but many have a greater impact on the region, and cleaning up these sites offers little benefit. But communities that are determined to control and manage growth avoid burdening future generations with a costly and debilitating legacy.

Sustainability also increases the economic value of place. In *Urban Fortunes*, Logan and Molotch explore the concept. According to them, the value of place increases not only as a result of property ownership but also as a result of the efforts made by people to develop their communities and resources. People need a roof, walls and space to make a life. How they choose (if they are able) a locale and housing is often the result of chance and available means. If people are comfortable in their neighborhood, they bond with it and develop an emotional attachment. Although a number of things (food, a local hangout or shared ethnic identity) can create this emotional attachment, Phillip Roth suggests that childhood experience may be the most common explanation: "Perhaps by definition a neighborhood is the place to which a child spontaneously gives undivided attention...That's the unfiltered way meaning comes to children, just flowing off the surface of things."

Although people have the ability to relocate, actually moving is not quite as simple. Places are "machinations," usually created or built. They can be developed, perhaps, by a corner market that offers kosher food, a street fair or parade or a backyard barbecue. Neighborhoods can organize watches to keep kids safe. But that does not mean people are fully satisfied. Neighborhoods usually want more: parks, a playground, a school or better streets. So places are not exempt from the public domain; people want their places improved. And that's where the commoditization of property enters the political economy.

No one ever promised that life would be fair. Any commodity has value, and the market determines that value. As a town grows, its bank buys the prized corner lot and the auto garage moves to a less highly valued location. After all, the bank serves more people and is therefore more important. It also has more money. Place is important, and it is rarely comparable. The growth of the city is not simply an economic process or even reducible to political economy; it is the product of human action and interaction, the strategies of leaders, groups and individuals and the ways their endeavors succeed or fail in the course of history. North Jersey provides innumerable examples of this reality. The home rule tradition, the "multiple municipal madness" described by Alan Karcher and the willingness to partner with others to attempt larger enterprises all reflect the determination of the people of North Jersey to adapt their "place" to provide the living conditions and experience they desire.

LOCAL OR NOMAD?

For many people, the local is an important cornerstone of life. In *The Lure of the Local* (1997), Lucy Lippard describes the importance of the concept of local as the geophysical component of the psychological "need to belong somewhere." Place is at the center of this drive, as it is a location that is known and familiar to the individual. It is therefore subjective—the product of personal memory and history. Its meaning can inspire the artist, as well as the community activist. But as Lippard points out, location is not universally a happy place. For many, it can be traumatic or bittersweet. For some, a high school reunion is a "never miss" event, while others feel that the thought of such a reunion is far too painful to contemplate.

Place is not limited to a small town or a neighborhood. Industrial sites, farms or other workplaces may be seen as alternatives, depending on what meaning the individual gives them. Geography and environment are powerful influences on human development. Consider the differences in perception and behavior between people who were raised in a coastal fishing village and those who grew up in the Highlands. The more distinctive a place is, the more it has a profound impact on people's memory. Another example is the different responses to place between monocultural locals and multicentered "nomads." Many people, from modest workers to highly educated professionals, live out their lives in one locale for a variety of reasons. In North Jersey, it may be inheriting a home (homeownership is an inaccessible luxury for many in this region) that governs their lives by tying them to their hometowns. Approximately half of the area's college-bound students attend institutions in other states, but many of these students return to the area to pursue their chosen careers. Strong ethnic and religious family ties also bind people to a region. Whatever the determining factor, many North Jerseyans complete their life cycles within a small territorial radius and generally do not think much about the matter. Newcomers have more choice in selecting their locale. They are often drawn to an area by jobs or the likelihood of a better one. Oftentimes, however, newcomers who are busy with work and family never penetrate the local scene and certainly not within their first year of living in a new place. This writer can testify to that behavior. I have lived in nineteen towns in six states for at least a year. But after one establishes a familiarity with an area and its establishments, organizations, institutions, people and culture, place takes on more personal meaning and significance.

TESTIMONY OF THE CREATIVE

Now and again, someone gives voice to the meaning of the locale in his or her life. It can take many forms, from artistic rendering to essay, poem or story, to other forms of testimony. A few examples from the immense reservoir available will have to suffice for North Jersey at this point. One generalization is offered: these creative people viewed North Jersey as a place, a unique place, with an appreciative eye. They reported or articulated—either in word or image—what they saw, with an open or even positive perspective. Some would become critical of society or economy or politics over time but would usually have relocated to New York or elsewhere by that point. This is not always the case. Many writings are negative, emphasizing corruption or weirdness or other negatives. A recent version is a collection by noted novelist Joyce Carol Oates on *New Jersey Noir*. It is an interesting question that deserves further study, but for now, here are some examples.

Perhaps the most profound and enduring testimony regarding North Jersey as a place is the poetry of William Carlos Williams. A doctor by profession and poet by inspiration, Williams lived out his life in Rutherford, a small Bergen County town that had fewer than five thousand people at the turn of the century. In his epic poem "Paterson," which was published in four volumes between 1946 and 1958, Williams presents the declining city as somewhere that could be everywhere and people—real and imaginary—of worth and character living in a place of remarkable interest, despite the fact that it was awash in closed factories and buildings. The account is a real story about ordinary people in an unordinary place. Williams's own hometown in Rutherford was too small and lacked the industrial setting Paterson had, while New York was too large. Even after writing the poem, Williams kept

The Great Falls, Paterson. *Photo by author.*

returning to the city and the topic, keeping notes to write a future volume on the nature of Paterson and its people.

A complementary (though unconnected) photographic essay of the city by George Tice appeared in 1972, and an updated version appeared in 2006. The book, also labeled simply *Paterson,* includes images of the beautiful Great Falls and glimpses of the adjacent mountain and river, as well as downtown structures, bars and street scenes featuring everyday people struggling with their everyday lives. Explanatory notes in this photographic essay reveal that while both artists looked at the city with a hard, unfiltered eye, both felt deeply about the historic town and the travails of its long-suffering inhabitants.

Another highly regarded photographic essay is Dan Graham's "Homes for America," which was published in *Arts Magazine* in 1966–67. This essay captures the uniform and inelegant mass-produced postwar homes that cluttered the suburbs of North Jersey in the 1960s. But Graham treated this subject with respect rather than with disdain. His interest was in the landscape and how it was changing. He presented his subject as something of interest and not something deserving of ridicule.

Robert Smithson, a friend of Graham's, wrote "A Tour of the Monuments of Passaic, New Jersey" (Passaic was a one-time industrial town between Rutherford and Paterson) in 1967. His "monuments" included a bridge that crossed over the Passaic River, a pumping station in the middle of the river and an enormous underutilized downtown parking lot. He found something eternal in this formless suburb, which he described as a "negative entity of formlessness [that] displaces the center which is the city and then swamps the country."

There are many North Jersey artists and performers but far more writers. The tracks left by James Fenimore Cooper, Stephen Crane and Phillip Roth take us by the hand and allow us to see North Jersey from a different perspective—from their perspective. Roth, for example, grounds much of his writing in troubled Newark and focuses mostly on the community of Weequahic, the middle-class Jewish neighborhood where he grew up. The Jewish experience pervades much of his work, particularly *Goodbye Columbus* and *American Pastoral*, though the latter has even more extensive grounding in the villages—and class distinctions—of rural Morris County, where his hero Swede Levov buys a country estate in his quest to realize the American dream.

Frederick Reiken also spins a tale of identity and coming of age in North Jersey in *The Lost Legends of New Jersey*. He develops several characters, so the experiences narrated in his work are spread among multiple participants. But many dimensions of the North Jersey experience are there: the familiar diner; summertime at the shore; getting lost on the winding narrow roads of the Meadowlands and finding unimaginable discards there (in this case, the instruments and uniforms of a high school band); the awesome New York skyline; and the poetry of William Carlos Williams. He comments on the abundance of natural landmarks and features, such as the abandoned Shale Hill Quarry at Roseland and the South Mountain Reservation, a 2,147-acre woodlands in Essex County. He discusses the ethnic divisions and separations of older generations from newer ones and examines the looming question of identity and legend and how they relate to current experiences of residents. It is not the places that matter here but the people and the shared experience that defines them. Following is an excerpt from *Lost Legends*:

> *And always Anthony wanted answers. He wanted some logical story to explain why she* [his mother] *was gone. So he invented the explanations. He tried to think of her the way he thought of characters in legends.*
>
> *But he was always doing that, making things up, trying to see how it all might fit into a legend. He didn't understand why he did this, because New Jersey was not legend. It was the armpit of America, according to most people. Still he saw everything around him as a legend.*

Many people live in North Jersey, and some move away. Some from both groups provide testimonials, and many of these have been published. A collection of such pieces (which are often found by serendipitous means on library shelves) was collected and edited by Irina Reyn, who just so happened to be a newcomer to North Jersey. She gathered a fascinating batch of twenty essays, memoirs and tales of New Jersey, all of which were centered around the New Jersey Turnpike or Garden State Parkway. At least half of these pieces are about North Jersey, and all vary in theme, but all are personal and touch, in one way or another, on identity or the importance of place. Bruce Springsteen is a frequent touchstone through the volume; his music also revolves around sense of place. His verses capture the feelings of New Jersey's youth; but the book also incorporates other themes, such as movement, travel, escaping New Jersey and commuting from Hoboken.

Her *Living on the Edge of the World* theme is actually a poor descriptor, as Reyn herself notes: "The 'edge of the world' it seems, turned out to be more essential, more invigorating than any center could have been. The place theme shows up some of the stories about the inability to get away from

Jersey even after leaving or in the rich descriptions of little-known places like Hillside, Jersey City, Cranford or Fort Lee. The short pieces enrich and confirm themes from longer novels by Roth or Reiken. North Jersey is a place that is not always loved but difficult to forget or escape mentally even if physically accomplished; it has an identity, and though it is not always pretty, it's certainly distinctive.

What is it that stimulates such creativity? Is it the access to New York publishers? The powerful relationship North Jersey has with Gotham is constantly felt, and yet, there is something special and unique that dwellers find in this special place. And they continuously express that sense of it vividly in poem, novel, song and film.

The use of literature, art and folklore allows expressions and understandings of place that social science can only wish for. Typically, the scholar utilizes employment or per capita income, political participation, air or water pollution or other quantifiable data to express quality of life issues and the emotional side of place in people's lives. This is unsatisfactory as a method of assessing the cultural, emotional and interactive dimension, and scholars are often left to conduct further research. But the experience embedded in creative expression can serve as data as well. Only humans can capture and share the never-ending story of the human experience.

CONCLUSION

Now that we have concluded our tour in search of North Jersey, what did we learn? While information has been provided regarding the questions, the answers rest ultimately with the reader. Is North Jersey really a specific place distinct from the rest of the state and from New York City?

Clearly, I've shown such is the case. It is separate from New York politically but not economically, and there exists a partnership between the two areas and not a dependency. North Jersey is separate from South Jersey economically and culturally because of its lack of identity resulting from New York's media influence. It was this identity issue that initiated the inquiry. North Jersey is burdened with a negative image that is widespread in the region and even across the country. It's an image of corruption, overcrowding, urban decay and violence, pollution, monotonous suburbs, overtaxation and cultural backwardness, and these images are fostered by the New York media. Some area residents share these perceptions despite the fact that most, if opinion surveys are to be believed, like living here.

The study uncovered other unresolved issues:

- Is North Jersey's image valid? Are there alternatives to these negative perceptions? How corrupt is the area? How polluted? What is the potential and future of its cities?

- How do residents really feel about the area? Are they just perched here temporarily for career advancement or other reasons? Or are they committed to the region?
- Who controls North Jersey? New Jersey overall has a notable "business friendly" reputation. Considering all the corporate headquarters located in the north section of the state, are there fiscal reasons as to why businesses chose to locate or remain here? Does business exercise too much influence over public policy?
- With its sharp divide between rich and poor, is there any chance of creating genuine community?

Finding North Jersey provides background for considering these questions. The answers, however, require further exploration of the issues presented in this book, as well as the input of the people of North Jersey. These matters can be surveyed while, hopefully, avoiding the pitfalls of political debate and competition. Such information gathering begins with the reader or interested citizen, and the information gleaned can add to the discussion and study on the nature and identity of this region and help bring about collaboration and consideration of its issues and strategies for the future.

Please join the endeavor to improve the perceptions and increase the appreciation of North Jersey.

NOTES ON SOURCES

Authors of important works on New Jersey history include John Cunningham, Thomas Fleming, Maxine Lurie and Michael Mappen. Larger issues and themes must necessarily be considered to understand the subject of this study. The author found works by Manuel Castells, Richard Florida, David Harvey and Lewis Mumford to be particularly illuminating in perceiving the larger issues at work in North Jersey society.

For information on New Jersey's geography, see Charles Stansfield's *A Geography of New Jersey*; for politics, see Barbara and Stephen Salmore's *New Jersey Politics and Government*.

The *Encyclopedia of New Jersey* is a good resource for many issues, and Wikipedia is a good starting place for learning about something unfamiliar.

CHAPTER 1

Some of the ideas included in this chapter come from Beck's *Tales and Towns of Northern New Jersey*; Hayes-Conroy's *South Jersey Under the Stars*; Coté's *Jersey Boys*; Cumbler's *A Social History of Economic Decline*; *The Hidden Dimension* by Hall; *Strangers in a Strange Land* by Massey; *A Geography of New Jersey* by Stansfield; and *In Gotham's Shadow* by Thomas.

Chapter 2

For information on "white Indians," see *American Encounters*, pages 483–85. For information on the iron plantations, see Rutsch and Gowalski's article "The Colonial Plantation Settlement Pattern in New Jersey." For more on immigration to North Jersey, see *Daily Life in Immigrant America* by Berquist (for Germans); *New Jersey Immigrant Experience* by Cunningham; *Enduring Community* by Helmreich (for Jews); *American Immigration* by Jones; *Asian-Americans* by Min and *Asian American Dreams* by Zin. For more on Newark, see Price's *Beleaguered City As Promised Land* and Wright's *New Place*. For more information on the Irish, refer to *The Irish in New Jersey* by Quinn; see Starr on the *Italians*. Espenshade's *Successful Immigration* and Montalto's *Out of the Many, One* are useful for learning more about immigrant integration in the region. Resources on women's working conditions include Clemens, DeLima, Sayels and Weatherford. Portes and Rumbaut provide a good overview, and the article "Immigration Theory for a New Century: Some Problems and Opportunities" by Portes is important for the adaptation of recent immigrants. For more on the area's Indian community, see Kalita's *Suburban Sahibs*.

Chapter 3

For the history of the state, see Cunningham, Fleming, Lurie and Mappen. Pink offers a macro view of the importance of story in one of his chapters in *A Whole New Mind*. For more on the importance of story in regard to place, see Daiute and Lightfoot's *Narrative Analysis*. Collections of Jersey stories are popular as a genre as the *Weird New Jersey* series and numerous anthologies—such as those edited by Blackwell, Lurie and Mappen—indicate. McConville's *Daring Disturbers* and Pomfret's *East New Jersey* offer a good overview of early colonial disputes between New Jersey and New York. A laudatory history of business development and innovation in the state is provided in *History of Ingenuity and Industry in New Jersey* by Johnson. For a commercial update on North Jersey, see Carascio's *Northern New Jersey*. On corporate research, see Pierce and Reich; for other perspectives, see Audretsch's *Innovation*, Brown and Duguid's *Social Life of Information* and

Gibbons's *New Production of Knowledge.* For more on home rule, see Trafford's "Home Rule." Cavanaugh recounts the Great Swamp story, while Quinn provides a distinctive artist's view of the Meadowlands.

CHAPTER 4

In their text *New Jersey Politics and Government,* the Salmores treat the state as a product of the suburban phenomenon. Other titles on suburbanization include Duany's *Suburban Nation;* Hayden's studies of *Suburbia* and *Sprawl;* Jackson's *Crabgrass Frontier;* and Stilgoe's *Borderland.* Rubey presents arguments against Jackson's theory in a collection on *Redefining Suburban Studies.* Lang similarly critiques Garreau's "edge city" in *Edgeless Cities.* Cohen's *Consumers Republic* and the Pratts' "The Impact of Some Regional Shopping Centers" examine the impact of the shopping malls in North Jersey and the emerging consumer society. For other economic factors, see Stanbeck, *Transforming Metropolitan Economy.* For grander mega-city ideas, see Brugmann (*Urban Revolution*), Glaeser (*Triumph of the City*) and Knox (*Metroburbia*). For the influence of digital, network and collaborative technologies, see Bingham and Conner (*Social Learning*), Castells (*Rise of the Network Society*), Mitchell (*Me++*) and Weinberger (*Everything Is Miscellaneous*). For meso-level opportunities and learning, see Boekema (*Knowledge, Innovation*), Brown and Duguid (*Social Life of Information*) and Florida (*Creative Class* and *Who's Your City*).

CHAPTER 5

Wacker (*Musconetcong Valley*) and *History of Morris County* provide background on the Morris Canal. Cranmer (*New Jersey in the Automobile Age*), Lovero (*Hudson County*), Stilgoe (*Metropolitan Corridor* and *Train Time*), Treese (*Railroads of New Jersey*) and Wolf (*Crossing the Hudson*) are all useful sources for the themes of this chapter. *America's Auto Dealers: The Master Merchandisers* is helpful in understanding the role of auto dealers. See Flink (*Automobile Age*) and Kay (*Asphalt Nation*) on the impact of the automobile. On regionalism, Benjamin and Nathan provide an important study. Doig's *Empire on the*

Hudson: Entrepreneurial Vision and Political Power at the Port of New York Authority offers the definitive study of the Port Authority.

CHAPTER 6

For place, *Place Matters* by Drier and his colleagues is important; Briney's discussion of Cristaller's work is helpful for "central place theory," while Florida articulates new conceptions of the importance of place for one's career and development in *Who's Your City*. For more on Montville, see Colrick (*Montville*) and Shults (*Moonlight Over the Canal*). Norwood and Murphy are good sources of information on Paterson. Scranton provides one of the best accounts of the 1913 silk strike in Paterson, as do both Golin and Tripp. Useful accounts of Newark are available in Galishoff, Kevin Mumford and Porambo. Alex Marshall is a keen observer of the workings of the city. Tuan explains topophilia. Influential works on sustainability, selected among many, include McDonough and Braungart (*Cradle to Cradle*), Milbrath (*Envisioning a Sustainable Society*) and Senge (*Necessary Revolution*). For efforts to conserve open lands in New Jersey, see Hiscano. Power's *Lost Landscapes* is useful for another perspective on the workings of local economies. See Tice for the photographic treatments of Paterson. For literary illustrations, see Buckley (*Tramps Like Us*), Reiken (*Lost Legends of New Jersey*), Roth (*American Pastoral*) and Williams (*Paterson*). Also see the collections by Broderick (*Paging New Jersey*) and the titles *Jerseyana* (Mappen), *Living on the Edge* (Reyn) and *What's Your Exit?* (Vallese).

BIBLIOGRAPHY

Audretsch, David B. *Innovation and Industrial Evolution.* Cambridge, MA: MIT Press, 1995.

Barone, Michael. *The New Americans.* Washington, D.C.: Regnery, 2001.

Bebout, John E., and Ronald J. Grele. *Where Cities Meet: The Urbanization of New Jersey.* Princeton, NJ: D. Van Nostrand, 1964.

Beck, Henry Charlton. *Tales and Towns of Northern New Jersey.* New Brunswick, NJ: Rutgers University Press, 1983.

Benjamin, Gerald, and Michael P. Nathan. *Regionalism and Realism: A Study of Government in the New York Metropolitan Area.* New York: Brookings, 2001.

Berquist, James M. *Daily Life in Immigrant America, 1820–1870.* Westport, CT: Greenwood, 2008.

Bingham, Tony, and Marcia Conner. *The New Social Learning.* San Francisco: ASTD/Berrett–Koehler, 2010.

Blackwell, Jon. *Notorious New Jersey: 100 True Tales of Murders and Mobsters Scandals and Scoundrels.* New Brunswick, NJ: Rivergate, 2008.

Boekema, Frans, et al. *Knowledge, Innovation and Economic Growth: The Theory and Practice of Learning Regions.* Cheltenham, England: Edward Elgar, 2001.

Brianculli, Aanthony J. *Iron Rails in the Garden State: Tales of New Jersey Railroading.* Bloomington: University of Indiana Press, 2008.

Briney, Amanda. "An Overview of Christaller's Central Place Theory." About.com. Accessed January 7, 2012. http://geography.about.com/od/urbaneconomicgeography/a/centralplace.htm.

Broderick, James F. *Paging New Jersey: A Literary Guide to the Garden State.* New Brunswick, NJ: Rutgers University Press, 2003.

Brown, John Seely, and Paul Duguid. *The Social Life of Information.* Boston: Harvard Business School Press, 2008.

Brugmann, Jeb. *Welcome to the Urban Revolution: How Cities Are Changing the World.* New York: Bloomsbury, 2009.

Buckley, Kristen. *Tramps Like Us: A New Jersey Tale.* London: Cyan, 2007.

Caracio, Judyann R. *Northern New Jersey: Gateway to the World Marketplace.* Northridge, CA: Windsor, 1998.

Castells, Manuel. *The Rise of the Network Society.* 2nd ed. Vol. 1. Malden, MA: Blackwell, 2008.

Cavanaugh, Cam. *Saving the Great Swamp: The People, the Power Brokers, and an Urban Wilderness.* Frenchtown, NJ: Columbia Publications, 1978.

Clemens, Paul G.E. *The Uses of Abundance: A History of New Jersey's Economy.* Trenton: New Jersey Historical Commission, Department of State, 1992.

Cohen, David Stephen, ed. *America: The Dream of My Life.* New Brunswick, NJ: Rutgers University Press.1990.

Cohen, Elizabeth. *A Consumer's Republic: The Politics of Mass Consumption in Postwar America.* New York: Knopf, 2003.

Colrick, Patricia F. *Montville.* Charleston, SC: Arcadia Publishing, 2000.

Coté, David. *Jersey Boys: The Story of Frankie Valli and the Four Seasons.* New York: Broadway Books, 2007.

County and City Extra: Annual Metro, City, and County Data Book. 17th ed. Lanham, MD: Bernan Press, 2009.

Cranmer, H. Jerome. *New Jersey in the Automobile Age.* Princeton, NJ: D. Van Nostrand, 1964.

Cumbler, John T. *A Social History of Economic Decline: Business, Politics, and Work in Trenton.* New Brunswick, NJ: Rutgers University Press, 1989.

Cunningham, Barbara, ed. *The New Jersey Immigrant Experience.* Union City, NJ: William H. Wise, 1997.

Cunningham, John T. *New Jersey: America's Main Road.* Revised ed. Garden City, NY: Doubleday, 1976.

———. *Railroads in New Jersey: The Formative Years.* Andover, NJ: Afton, 1997.

Daiute, Colette, and Cynthia Lightfoot, eds. *Narrative Analysis: Studying the Development of Individuals in Society.* Thousand Oaks, CA: Sage, 2004.

Danielson, Michael H., and Jameson W. Doig. *New York: The Politics of Urban Regional Development.* Berkeley: University of California Press, 1982.

DeLima, Agnes. *Nightworking Mothers in Textile Mills, Passaic, New Jersey.* N.p.: National Consumers League of New Jersey, 1920. http://nrs.harvard.edu/null?n=20. Accessed July 20, 2011. Digitized pamphlet.

Doig, Jameson W. *Empire on the Hudson: Entrepreneurial Vision and Political Power at the Port of New York Authority.* New York: Columbia University Press, 2001.

Dreier, Peter, Todd Swanstrom and John H. Mollenkopf, eds. *Place Matters: Metropolitics for the Twenty-First Century.* Revised ed. Lawrence: University Press of Kansas, 2005.

Duany, Andres, et al. *Suburban Nation.* New York: North Point, 2000.

Espenshade, Thomas J. *Keys to Successful Immigration: Implications of the New Jersey Experience.* Washington, D.C.: Urban Institute, 1997.

Evans, Hal. *They Made America.* New York: Little Brown, 2004.

Flam, Jack, ed. *Robert Smithson: The Collected Writings.* Berkeley: University of California Press, 1996.

Fleming, Thomas J. *New Jersey: A History.* New York: W.W. Norton, 1997.

Flink, James J. *The Automobile Age.* Cambridge, MA: MIT Press, 1998.

Florida, Richard. *The Rise of the Creative Class.* New York: Basic Books, 2002.

———. *Who's Your City?* New York: Basic Books, 2008.

Fogelson, Nancy. "They Paved the Streets with Silk: Paterson New Jersey Silk Workers, 1913–1924." *New Jersey History* 97, no. 1 (February 1979): 133–48.

Friedman, Thomas L. *The World Is Flat: A Brief History of the Twenty-first Century.* New York: Farrar, Straus & Giroux, 2004.

Gale, Dennis E. *Greater New Jersey: Living in the Shadow of Gotham.* Philadelphia: University of Pennsylvania Press, 2006.

Galishoff, Stuart. *Newark: The Nation's Unhealthiest City, 1830–1895.* New Brunswick, NJ: Rutgers University Press, 1975.

Garreau. Joe. *Edge City: Life on the New Frontier.* New York: Doubleday. 1998.

Ghemawat, Pankej. *World 3.0: Global Prosperity and How to Achieve It.* Boston: Harvard Business School Press, 2011.

Gibbons, Michael, et al. *The New Production of Knowledge: The Dynamics of Science and Research in Contemporary Societies.* London: Sage, 1994.

Gillespie, Angus Kress, and Michael Aaron Rockland. *Looking for America on the New Jersey Turnpike.* New Brunswick, NJ: Rutgers University Press, 1992.

Glaeser, Edward. *Triumph of the City.* New York: Penguin, 2011.

Golin, Steve. *The Fragile Bridge: Paterson Silk Strikes, 1913.* Philadelphia: Temple University Press, 1998.

Gottman, Jean. *Megalopolis: The Urbanized Northeastern Seaboard of the United States.* New York: Twentieth Century Fund, 1961.

Gottman, Jean, and Robert A. Harper, eds. *Since Megalopolis: The Urban Writings of Jean Goffman.* Baltimore, MD: Johns Hopkins University Press, 1990.

Graham, Dan. "Homes for America." *Arts Magazine,* 1966–1967. Available online.

Gruen, Dan, et al. "The Use of Stories in Experience Design." *International Journal of Human-Computer Interaction* 14, nos. 3 and 4: 503–34.

Hall, Edward T. *The Hidden Dimension.* New York: Random House, 1990.

Haller, William, Alejandro Portes and Scott M. Lynch. "Dreams Fulfilled, Dreams Shattered: Determinants of Segmented Assimilation in the Second Generation." *Social Forces* 89, no. 3 (March): 733–62.

Harvey, David. *The Enigma of Capital and the Crises of Capitalism.* New York: Oxford University Press, 2010.

———. *The Urbanization of Capital: Studies in the History and Theory of Capitalist Urbanization.* Baltimore, MD: Johns Hopkins University Press, 1985.

Hayden, Delores. *Building Suburbia: Greenfields and Urban Growth, 1820–2000.* New York: Vintage/Random House, 2003.

———. *A Field Guide to Sprawl.* New York: Norton, 2004.

———. "Power of Place." *International Encyclopedia of Social and Behavioral Science* 17. Oxford, England: Elsevier, 2001.

Hayes-Conroy, Allison. *South Jersey Under the Stars: Essays on Culture, Agriculture, and Place.* Madison, NJ: FDU Press, 2005.

Helmreich, William B. *The Enduring Community: The Jews of Newark and Metrowest.* New Brunswick, NJ: Transactions, 1990.

Hiscano, Dwight. *New Jersey: The Natural State.* New Brunswick, NJ: Rutgers University Press, 2000.

Hiss, Tony. *The Experience of Place.* New York: Alfred A. Knopf, 1990.

———. *In Motion: The Experience of Travel.* New York: Knopf, 2001.

Historical Statistics of the United States. Millennial edition. Vol. 3. New York: Cambridge University Press, 2006.

History of Morris County, New Jersey. New York: W.W. Munsell, 1878.

Jackson, Kenneth T. *Crabgrass Frontier: The Suburbanization of the United States.* New York: Oxford University Press, 1985.

Jacobs, Jane. *Cities and the Wealth of Nations.* New York: Random House, 1986.

———. *Death and Life of Great American Cities.* New York: Modern Library, 1969.

———. *The Economy of Cities.* New York: Vintage, 1970.

Johnson, James P. *New Jersey: History of Ingenuity and Industry.* N.p.: Windsor, 1987.

Jones, Maldwyn Allen. *American Immigration.* 2nd ed. Chicago: University of Chicago Press, 1992.

Kalita, S. Mitra. *Suburban Sahibs: Three Indian Families and Their Passage from India to America.* New Brunswick, NJ: Rutgers University Press, 2005.

Karcher, Alan J. *New Jersey's Multiple Municipal Madness.* New Brunswick, NJ: Rutgers University Press, 1998.

Kasarda, John, and Greg Lindsay. *Aerotropolis: The Way We'll Live Next.* New York: Farrar, Straus, and Giroux, 2011.

Kay, Jane Holtz. *Asphalt Nation.* New York: Crown, 1997.

Knox, Paul L. *Metroburbia, USA.* New Brunswick, NJ: Rutgers University Press, 2008.

Kuntsler, James Howard. *The Geography of Nowhere: The Rise and Demise of America's Manmade Landscape.* New York: Simon and Schuster, 1993.

Lang, Robert E. *Edgeless Cities: Exploring the Elusive Metropolis.* Washington, D.C.: Brookings, 2003.

Li, Wen. *Ethnoburbia: The New Ethnic Community in Urban America.* Honolulu: University of Hawaii Press, 2009.

Lingeman, Richard R. *Small Town America, 1620 to the Present.* New York: G.P. Putnam, 1980.

Lippard, Lucy R. *The Lure of the Local: Senses of Place in a Multicentered Society.* New York: New Press 1997.

Logan, John R., and Harvey L. Molotch. *Urban Fortunes: The Political Economy of Place.* Berkeley: University of California Press, 1987.

Lovero, Joan Doherty. *Hudson County: The Left Bank.* Sun Valley, CA: American Historical Press, 1999.

Lurie, Maxine, ed. *A New Jersey Anthology.* New Brunswick, NJ: Rutgers University Press, 1994.

Lurie, Maxine, and Marc Mappen, eds. *Encyclopedia of New Jersey.* New Brunswick, NJ: Rutgers University Press, 2004.

Lurie, Maxine, and P. Wacker, eds. 2009. *Mapping New Jersey: An Evolutionary Landscape*. New Brunswick, NJ: Rivergate, 2009.

Mancall, Peter C., and James H. Merrill, eds. *American Encounters: Natives and Newcomers from European Contact to Indian Removal, 1500–1850*. 2nd ed. New York: Routledge, 2007.

Mappen, Marc. *Jerseyanna: The Underside of New Jersey History.* New Brunswick, NJ: Rutgers University Press, 1994.

Mariani, Paul. *William Carlos Williams: A New World Naked*. New York: McGraw Hill, 1981.

Marshall, Alex. *How Cities Work: Suburbs, Sprawl, and the Roads Not Taken*. Austin: University of Texas Press, 2000.

Massey, Douglas S. *Strangers in a Strange Land: Humans in an Urbanizing World*. New York: W.W. Norton, 2005.

McConville, Brendan. *Those Daring Disturbers of the Public Peace: The Struggle for Property and Power in Early New Jersey*. Ithaca: Cornell University Press, 1999.

McCormick, Richard P., and Katheryne C. McCormick. *Equality Deferred: Women Candidates for New Jersey Assembly, 1920–1993*. New Brunswick, NJ: Rutgers University, 1994.

McDonough, William, and Michael Braungart. *Cradle to Cradle: Remaking the Way We Make Things*. New York: North Point Press, 2002.

Meyrowitz, Jacob. *No Sense of Place: The Impact of Electronic Media on Social Behavior*. New York: Oxford University Press, 1985.

Milbrath, Lester W. *Envisioning a Sustainable Society: Learning Our Way Out*. Albany: State University of New York Press, 1989.

Min, Pyong Gap. *Asian-Americans: Contemporary Trends and Issues*. 2nd ed. Thousand Oaks, CA: Pine Forge/Sage, 2006.

Mitchell, William J. *City of Bits: Space, Place and the Infobahn.* Cambridge, MA: MIT Press, 1995.

———. *Me ++: The Cyborg Self and the Networked City.* Cambridge, MA: MIT Press, 2004.

Molotch, Harvey. "Granite and Green: Thinking Beyond Surface in Place Studies." *Theory and Society* 40, no. 2 (December 2011): 155–59.

Molotch, Harvey, and William Freudenberg. "History Repeats Itself, But How? City Character, Urban Tradition, and the Accomplishment of Place." *American Sociological Review* 65, no. 6 (December 2000): 791–820.

Montalto, Nicholas V. *Out of the Many, One: Integrating Immigrants in New Jersey.* Washington, D.C.: National Immigration Forum, 2006.. PDF e-book.

Moss, Marie, and Barri Leiner Grant. *Jersey Girls: The Fierce and the Fabulous.* Philadelphia: Running Press, 2001.

Mumford, Kevin. *Newark: A History of Race, Rights, and Riots in America.* New York: NYU Press, 2007.

Mumford, Lewis. *The City in History.* New York: Harcourt Brace, 1967.

Murphy, J. Palmer, and Margaret Murphy. *Paterson and Passaic County: An Illustrated History.* Northridge, CA: Windham, 1987.

Nora, Pierre, ed. *Realms of Memory: Rethinking the French Past.* Vol. I. New York: Columbia University Press, 1996.

Norwood, Christopher. *About Paterson: The Making and Unmaking of an American City.* New York: E.P. Dutton, 1974.

Oates, Joyce Carol. *New Jersey Noir.* New York: Akashic Books, 2011.

Oldenburg, Ray. *The Great Good Place.* New York: Paragon, 1989.

Pelzer, B., et al., eds. *Dan Graham.* London: Phaidon Press, 2001.

Pierce, John R. Interview by H. Lyle, April 1979. Oral History Project, California Institute of Technology Archives. http://resolver.caltech.edu/CaltechOH:OH_Pierce_J.

———. "When Is Research the Answer?" *Science* 159, no. 3819 (March 1968): 1079–80.

Pierce, John R., and Arthur G. Tressler. *The Research State: A History of Science in New Jersey.* New Jersey Historical Society. Princeton: C. Van Nostrand, 1964.

Pindell, Terry. *A Good Place to Live: America's Last Migration.* New York: Owl/Henry Holt, 1995.

Pink, Daniel H. *A Whole New Mind.* New York: Riverhead, 2005.

Pomfret, John E. *The Province of East New Jersey, 1609–1720: The Rebellious Proprietorship.* Princeton, NJ: Princeton University Press, 1962

Pomper, Gerald M. "The Political State of New Jersey: Conclusion." In *A New Jersey Anthology*, edited by Lurie Maxine. New Brunswick, NJ: Rutgers University Press, 463–84.

Porambo, Ron. *No Cause for Indictment: An Autopsy of Newark.* New York: Holt, Rinehart, and Winston, 1971.

Portes, Alejandro. "Immigration Theory for a New Century: Some Problems and Opportunities." *International Migration Review* 31, no. 4 (Winter): 799–826.

Portes, Alejandro, and Rubin G. Rumbaut. *Immigrant America: A Portrait.* 2nd ed. Berkeley: University of California Press, 1996.

Power, Thomas Michael. *Lost Landscapes and Failed Economics: The Search for a Value of Place.* Washington, D.C.: Island Press, 1996.

Pratt, Samuel, and Lois Pratt. "The Impact of Some Regional Shopping Centers." *Journal of Marketing* 25, no. 2: 44–50.

Price, Clement A. *The Beleaguered City As Promised Land: Blacks in Newark, 1917–1947*. Trenton: New Jersey Historical Commission, 1975.

Quinn, Dermot. *The Irish in New Jersey*. New Brunswick, NJ: Rutgers University Press, 2004.

Quinn, John R. *Fields of Sun and Grass: An Artist's Journal of the New Jersey Meadowlands*. New Brunswick, NJ: Rutgers University Press, 1997.

Reich, Leonard S. *The Making of American Industrial Research: Science and Business at GE and Bell, 1876–1926*. Cambridge, MA: Cambridge University Press, 1985.

Reiken, Frederick. *The Lost Legends of New Jersey*. New York: Harcourt Brace, 2008.

Relph, Edward C. *The Modern Urban Landscape*. Baltimore, MD: Johns Hopkins University Press, 1997.

———. "Place in Geography." *International Encyclopedia of Social and Behavioral Science*. Vol. 17. Oxford, England: Elsevier, 2001.

Reyn, Irina, ed. *Living on the Edge of the World: New Jersey Writers Take on the Garden State*. New York: Touchstone, 2007.

Roberts, Manon, et al. "Place and Space in the Networked City: Conceptualizing the Integrated Metropolis." *Journal of Urban Design* 4, no. 1: 51–66.

Robinson, Eugene. *Disintegration: The Splintering of Black America*. New York: Doubleday, 2010.

Rockland, Michael Aaron. *The George Washington Bridge: Poetry in Steel*. New Brunswick, NJ: Rutgers University Press, 2008.

Roth, Philip. *American Pastoral*. New York: Vintage, 1997.

Rubey, Daniel, ed. *Redefining Suburban Studies: Searching for New Paradigms*. Hempstead, NY: Hofstra University, 2009.

Rutsch, Edward S. "The Colonial Plantation Settlement Pattern in New Jersey." In *Economic and Social History of Colonial New Jersey*. Trenton: New Jersey Historical Commission, 1974.

Ryden, Kent C. *Mapping the Invisible Landscape: Folklore, Writing, and the Sense of Place*. Iowa City: University of Iowa Press, 1993.

Salmore, Barbara G., and Stephen A. Salmore. *New Jersey Politics and Government*. 3rd ed. New Brunswick, NJ: Rutgers University Press, 2008.

Sayles, Mary B. *Housing Conditions in Jersey City*. Philadelphia: American Academy of Political and Social Science, 1903. PDF ebook.

Scranton, Philip B., ed. *Silk City: Studies in the Paterson Silk Industry, 1860–1940*. Newark: New Jersey Historical Society, 1985.

Senge, Peter, et al. *The Necessary Revolution: How Individuals and Organizations Are Working Together to Create a Sustainable World*. New York: Doubleday, 2008.

Shafer, Mary A. *Devastation on the Delaware*. Ferndale, PA: Word Forge, 2008.

Shults, Ruth. *Moonlight over the Canal*. Minneapolis: Mill City Press, 2006.

Siegel, Lee. "The Hidden State of Culture." *Wall Street Journal*, January 24, 2009. http:online.wsj.com/article/SB123275571425511845.html.

Spinella, Art, et al. *America's Auto Dealers: The Master Merchandisers*. Van Nuys, CA: Freed-Crown, 1978.

Stanbeck, Thomas M., Jr. *The Transforming Metropolitan Economy*. New Brunswick, NJ: Rutgers University Press, 2002.

Stansfield, Charles A., Jr. *A Geography of New Jersey: The City in the Garden*. New Brunswick, NJ: Rutgers University Press, 1998.

Starr, Dennis J. *The Italians of New Jersey*. Newark: New Jersey Historical Society, 1985.

Steinlieb, George, and Alex Schwartz. *New Jersey Growth Corridors.* New Brunswick, NJ: Rutgers University Press, 1986.

Stilgoe, John R. *Borderland: Origins of the American Suburb, 1820–1939.* New Haven, CT: Yale University Press, 1988.

———. *Metropolitan Corridor: Railroads and the American Scene.* New Haven, CT: Yale University Press, 1983.

———. *Train Time: Railroads and the Imminent Reshaping of the United States Landscape.* Charlottesville: University of Virginia Press, 2007.

Thomas, Alexander R. *In Gotham's Shadow: Globalization and Change in Central New York.* Albany: SUNY Press, 2003.

Tice, George A. *Paterson.* New Brunswick, NJ: Rutgers University Press, 1972.

———. *Paterson, II.* New York: Quantuck Lane Press, 2006.

Trafford, John E. "Home Rule in the '90s: Is It Alive or Dead?" New Jersey League of Municipalities. http://www.njslom.org/homerule.html.

Treese, Loret. *Railroads of New Jersey: Fragments of the Past in the Garden State Landscape.* Mechanicsburg, PA: Stackpole Books, 2006.

Tripp, Anne Huber. *The IWW and the Paterson Silk Strike of 1913.* Urbana: University of Illinois Press, 1987.

Tuan, Yi-Fu. *Topophilia: A Study of Environmental Perception, Attitudes and Values.* New York: Columbia University Press, 1990.

U.S. Bureau of Census. 2011. www.Census.gov/compendia/statab/2011/tables/11s0033.pdf.

Vallese, Joe, and A. Alicia Beale, eds. *What's Your Exit? A Literary Detour through New Jersey.* Middletown, NJ: Word Riot Press, 2010.

Vecol, Rudolph J. *The People of New Jersey.* Princeton, NJ: D. Van Nostrand, 1965.

Wacker, Peter O. *The Musconetcong Valley of New Jersey: A Historical Geography.* New Brunswick, NJ: Rutgers University Press, 1968.

Weatherford, Doris. *Foreign and Female: Immigrant Women in America, 1840–1930.* New York: Facts on File, 1995.

Weinberger, David. *Everything Is Miscellaneous: The Power of the New Digital Disorder.* New York: Times Books, 2007.

Whyte, William H. *City: Rediscovering the Center.* New York: Doubleday, 1998.

Williams, William Carlos. *Paterson.* Revised ed. Edited by C. MacGowan. New York: New Directions, 1992.

Wolf, Donald E. *Crossing the Hudson: Historic Bridges and Tunnels of the River.* New Brunswick, NJ: Rivergate, 2010.

Women in New Jersey Industries: A Study of Wages and Hours. Washington, D.C.: U.S. Department of Labor, Women's Bureau, 1924.

Worten, Stanley N. *Reshaping New Jersey: A History of Its Government and Politics.* Trenton: New Jersey Historical Commission, 1997.

WPA Guide to 1930s New Jersey. New Brunswick, NJ: Rutgers University Press, 1986.

Wright, Giles R. *Arrival and Settlement in a New Place.* Trenton: New Jersey Historical Commission, 1986.

Zia, Helen. *Asian American Dreams: The Emergence of an American People.* New York: Farrar, Straus, and Giroux, 2000.

About the Author

James W. Marcum is a professor and director of the Graduate School of Library and Information Studies at Queens College, City University of New York. A Texas native, he graduated with a PhD in history from the University of North Carolina–Chapel Hill. He has served as a library director for four different colleges and universities from Texas to New York, including the College of Staten Island CUNY and Fairleigh Dickinson University in North Jersey. He is the author of numerous scholarly articles and one book.

Visit us at
www.historypress.net